The Story of How Peter Became Pan

FINDING NEVERLAND

A New Broadway Musical

CONTENTS

ISBN 978-1-4950-7949-8

7777 W. Bluemound Rd. P.O. Box 13819 Milwaukee, WI 53213

In Australia Contact:
Hal Leonard Australia Pty. Ltd.
4 Lentara Court
Cheltenham, Victoria, 3192 Australia
Email: ausadmin@halleonard.com.au

Visit Hal Leonard Online at
www.halleonard.com

IF THE WORLD TURNED UPSIDE DOWN

Words and Music by ELIOT KENNEDY
and GARY BARLOW

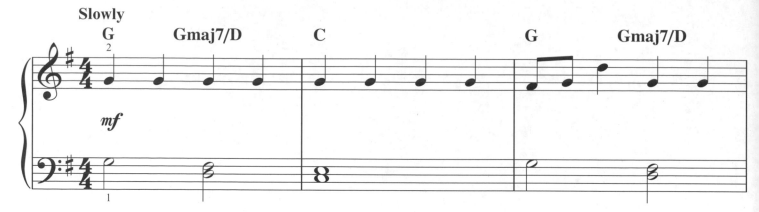

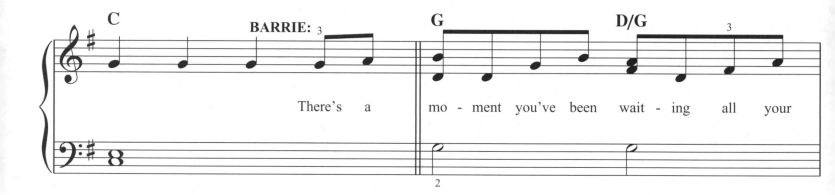

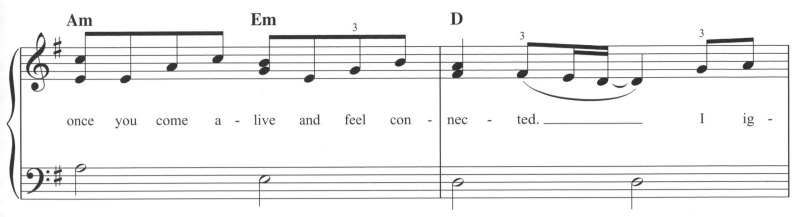

once you come a - live and feel con - nec - ted. _____ I ig -

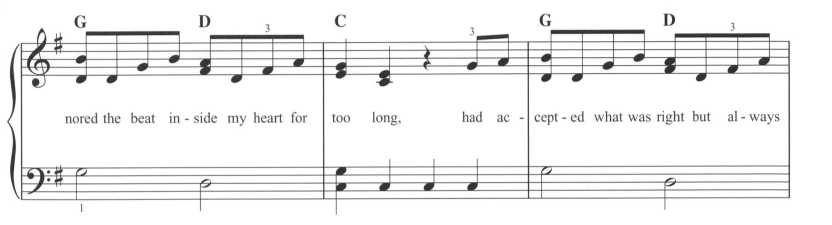

nored the beat in - side my heart for too long, had ac - cept - ed what was right but al - ways

felt wrong. It's the sec - ond hand of time I'd been a slave to, but in -

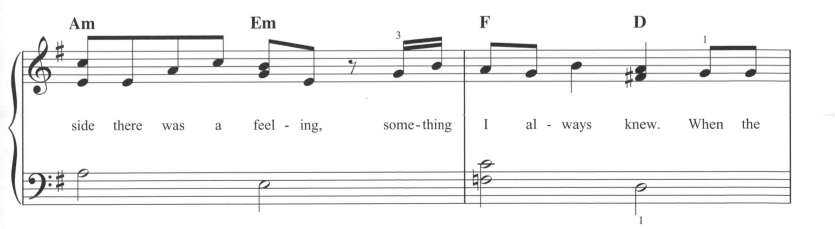

side there was a feel - ing, some - thing I al - ways knew. When the

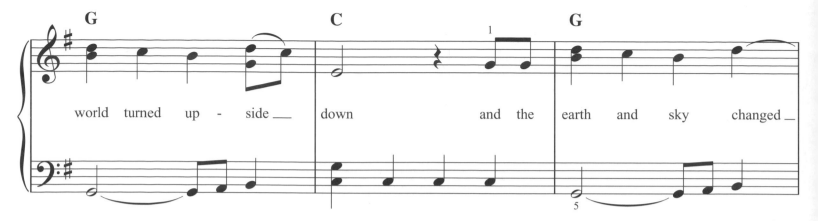

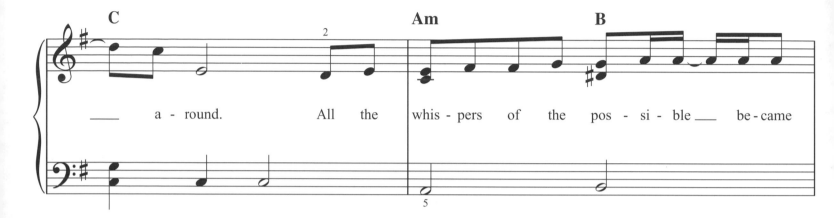

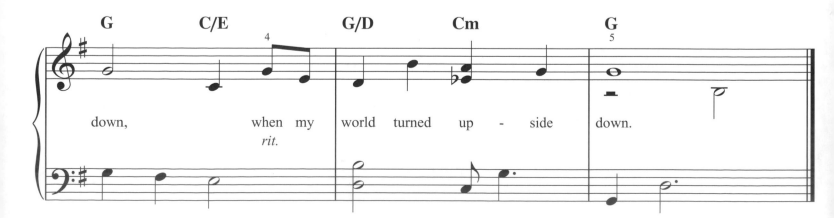

BELIEVE

Words and Music by ELIOT KENNEDY
and GARY BARLOW

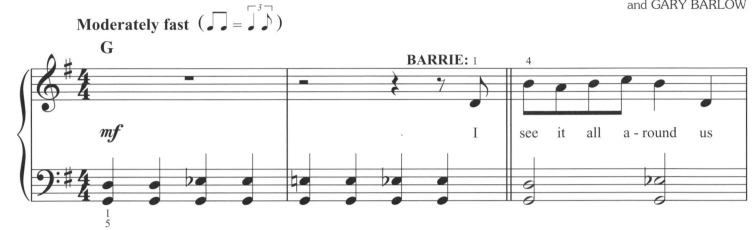

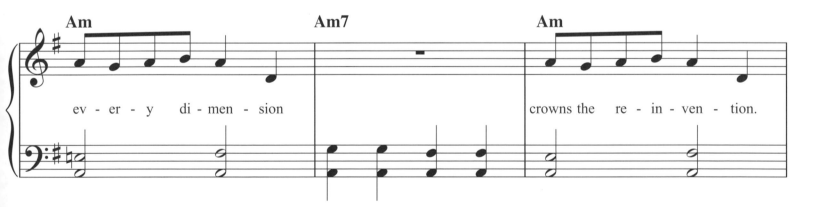

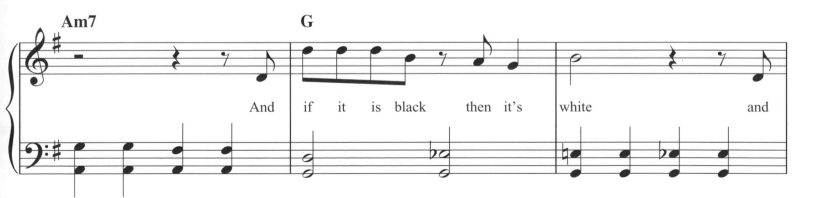

when it is dark then it's light. So fill in all the spa - ces

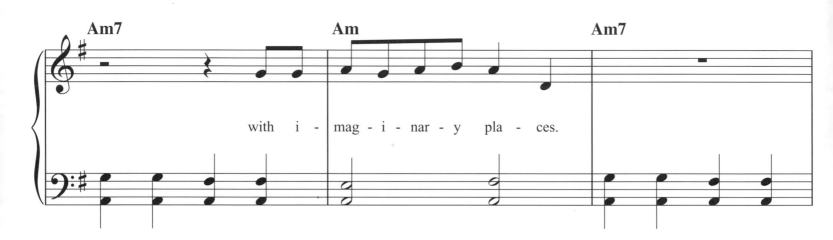

with i - mag - i - nar - y pla - ces.

It's so frus - tra - ting when no one else sees ev - 'ry - thing you

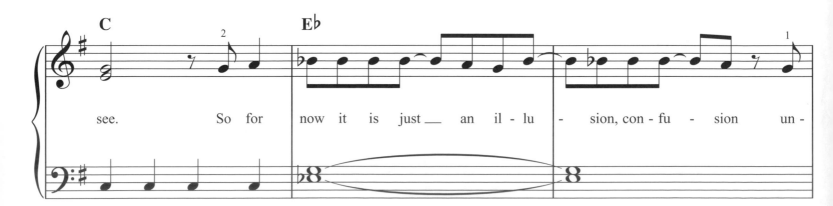

see. So for now it is just ___ an il - lu - sion, con - fu - sion un -

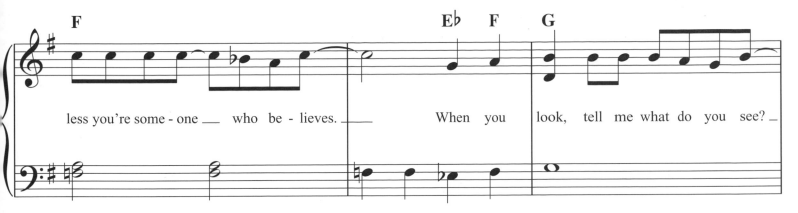

less you're some - one ___ who be - lieves. ___ When you look, tell me what do you see? ___

___ Just a dog in a park. Is it real? ___ Is it fic - tion, on - ly make be - lieve? You

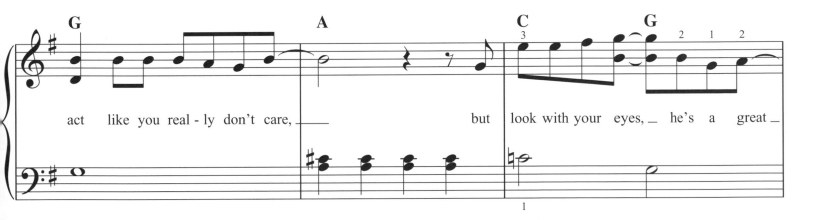

act like you real - ly don't care, ___ but look with your eyes, ___ he's a great ___

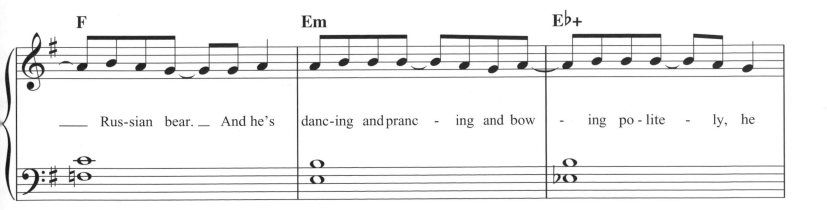

___ Rus-sian bear. ___ And he's danc-ing and pranc - ing and bow - ing po - lite - ly, he

plays to full hous - es once dai - ly, twice night - ly. Pre - fix 'or - di - na -

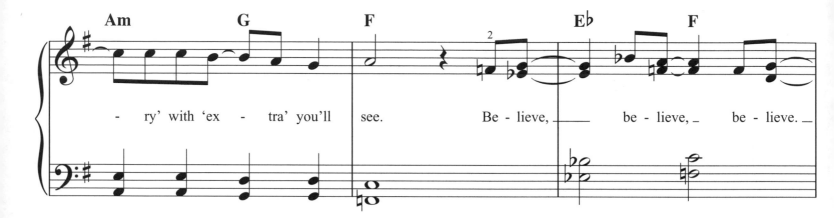

- ry' with 'ex - tra' you'll see. Be - lieve, _____ be - lieve, _ be - lieve. _

_____ I don't need rose - tint - ed spec - ta - cles

just to see the fun - da - men - tals. I

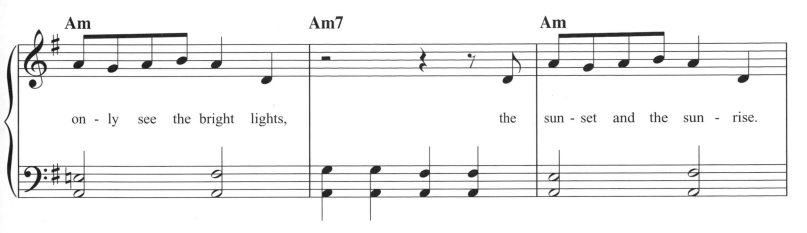

on - ly see the bright lights, the sun - set and the sun - rise.

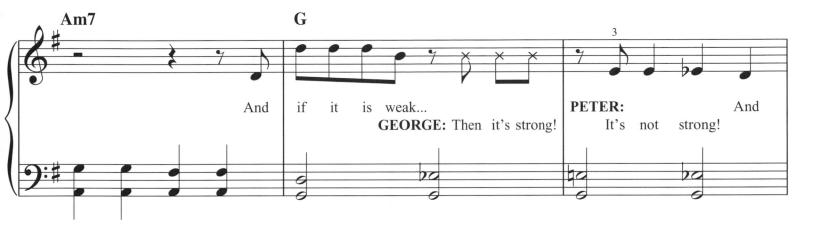

And if it is weak...
GEORGE: Then it's strong!

PETER: And
It's not strong!

BARRIE, SYLVIA & BOYS: 3

just when it's right...
GEORGE: Then it's wrong!

PETER: And
It's not wrong!

ev - 'ry - thing my eyes see...

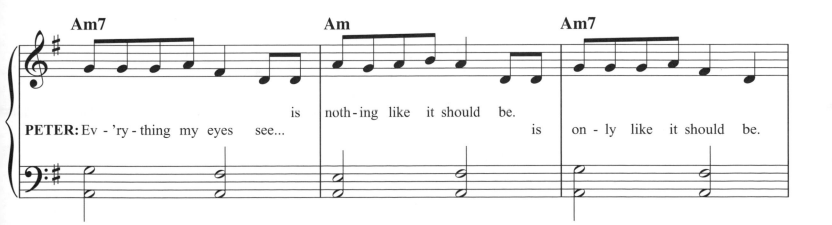

PETER: Ev - 'ry - thing my eyes see...
is noth - ing like it should be.
is on - ly like it should be.

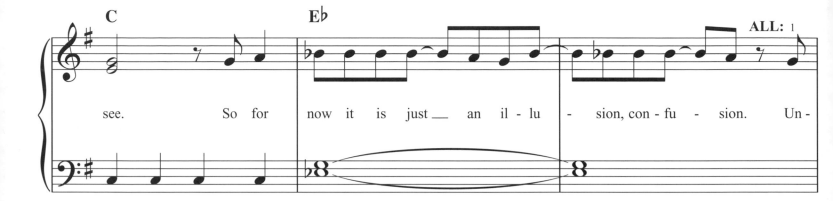

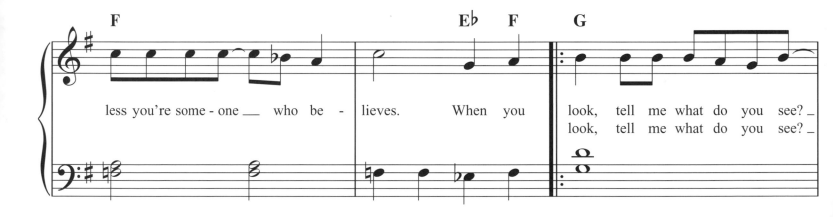

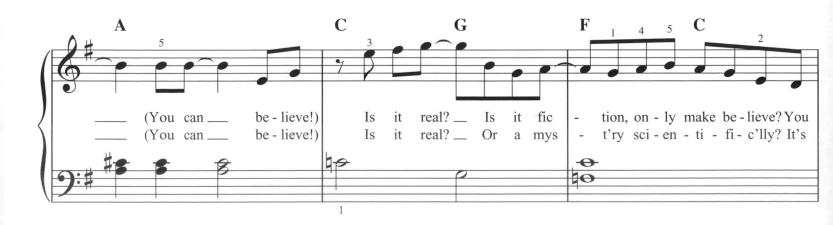

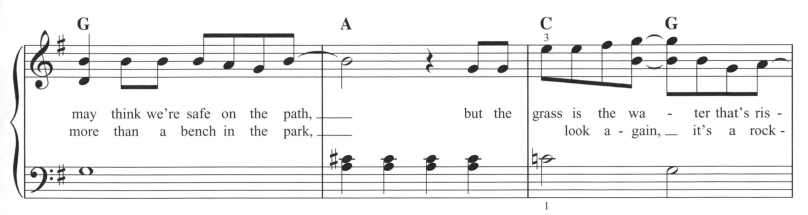

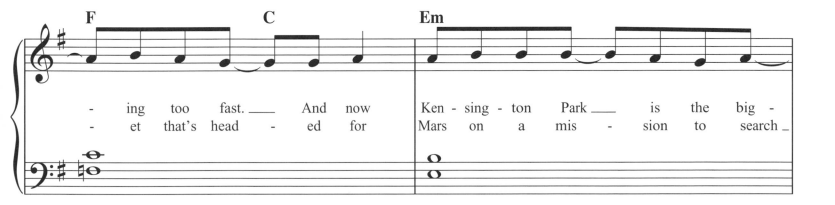

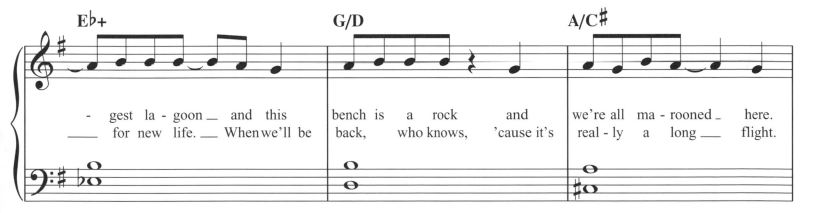

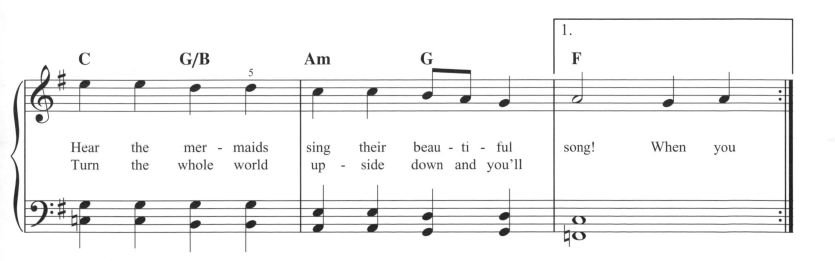

12

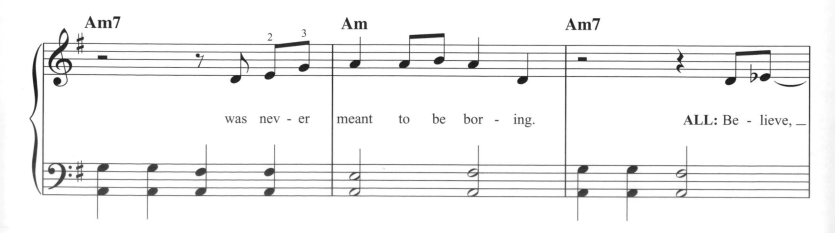

see.   Be - lieve, _____ be - lieve, _____ be - lieve. _____

BARRIE:

With just i - mag - i - na - tion   and cre -

a - tive spe - cu - la - tion.   Our life's call - ing

was nev - er meant to be bor - ing.   **ALL:** Be - lieve, _____

be - lieve, __ be - lieve, __ be - lieve, __ be - lieve, __ be - lieve, __ be - lieve, __

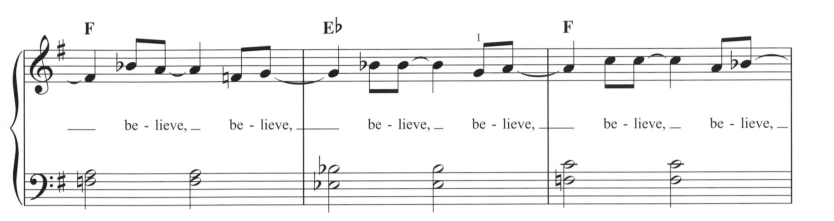

be - lieve, __ be - lieve, __ be - lieve, __ be - lieve, __ be - lieve, __ be - lieve, __

be - lieve, __ be - lieve, __ be - lieve. __ Be - lieve! __

WE OWN THE NIGHT

Words and Music by ELIOT KENNEDY
and GARY BARLOW

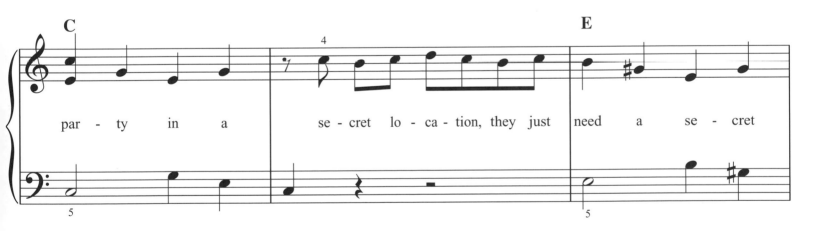

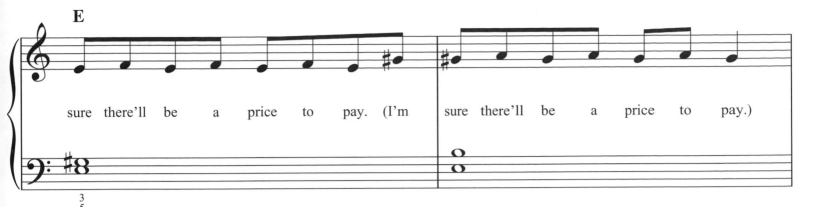

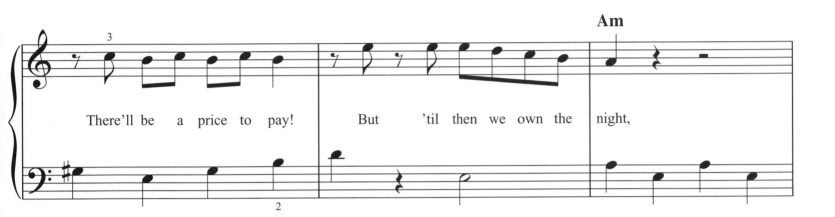

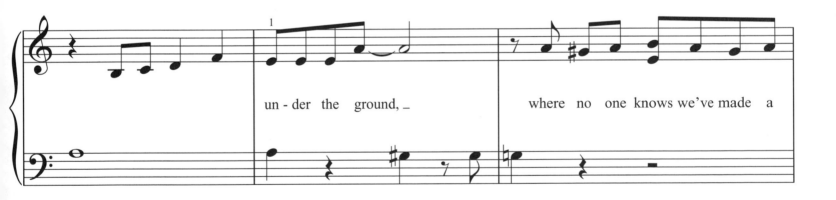

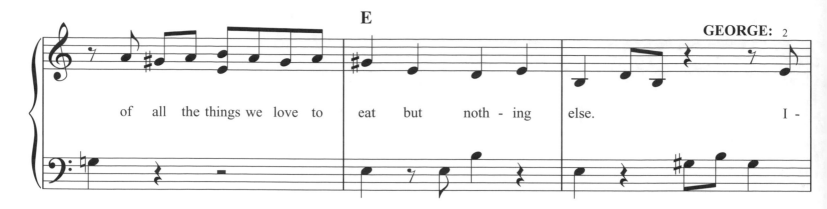

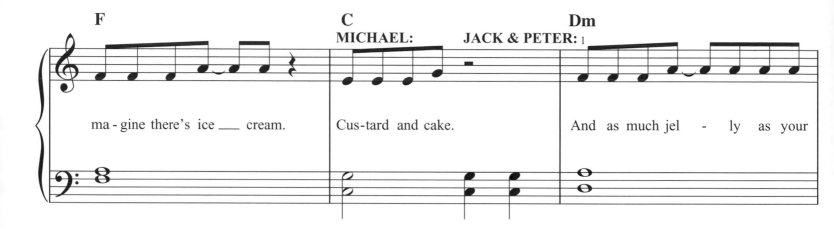

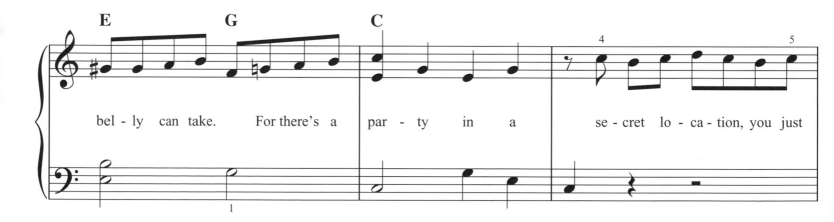

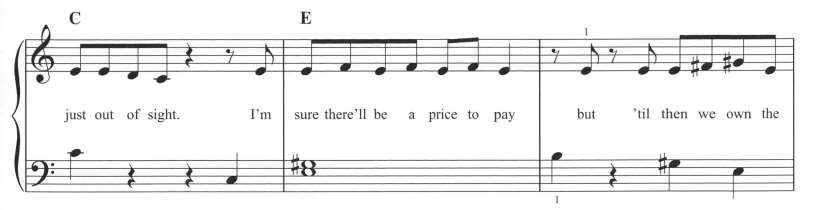

just out of sight. I'm sure there'll be a price to pay but 'til then we own the

night. Oh, how we love this mad - ness,

so en - ter - tain - ing, we'll be shar - ing glad - ness, they'll be com-plain-ing. We'll be

right un - der their nos - es but we're just out of sight. I'm sure there'll be a price to pay. (I'm
cresc.

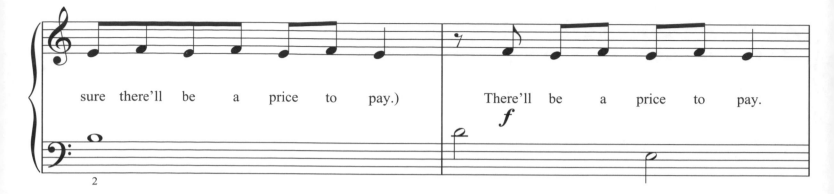

STRONGER

Words and Music by ELIOT KENNEDY
and GARY BARLOW

li - vers me,   I don't need __ their sym - pa - thy.

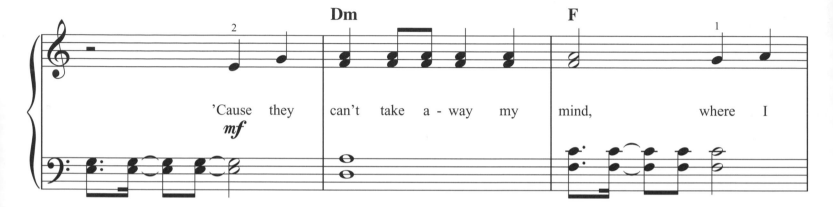

'Cause they can't take a - way my   mind,   where I

go they will nev - er   find.   I've got to __ be

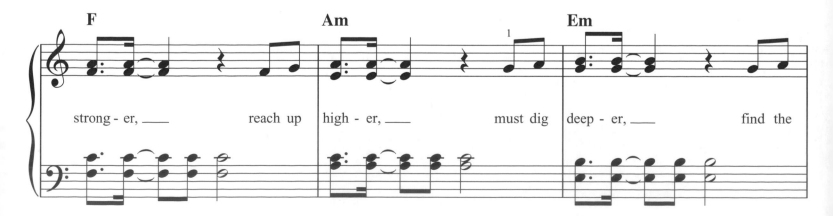

strong - er, ___   reach up high - er, ___   must dig deep - er, ___   find the

23

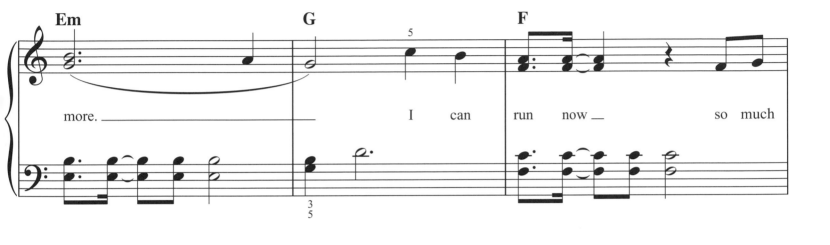

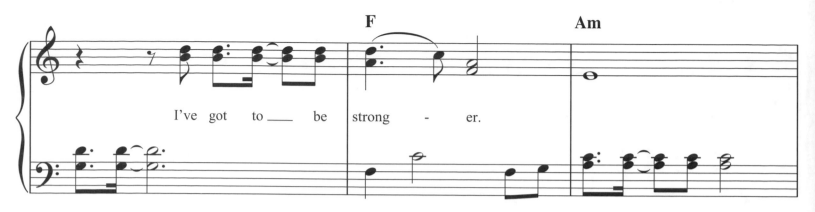

I've got to ___ be strong - er.

Oh. _____

HOOK:

You'll see ___ in time

you will ___ sur - vive,   too soon ___ to run   too late ___ to hide. It's

your des - ti - ny,   ev - er - y pace, ev - 'ry   stride.

cresc.

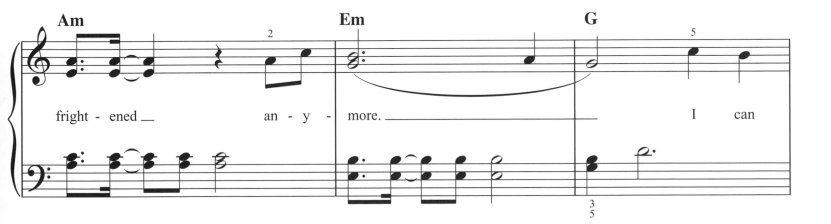

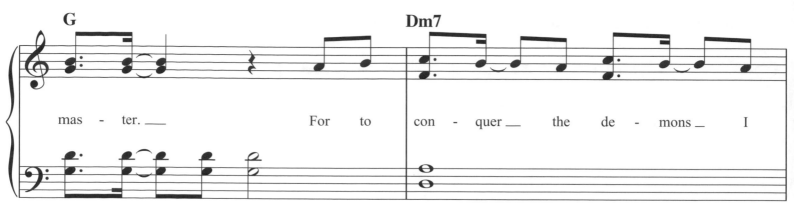

mas - ter. ___ For to con - quer ___ the de - mons ___ I

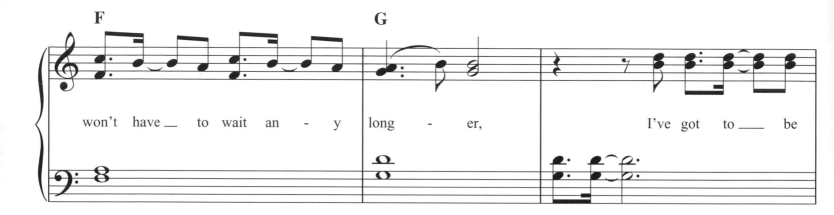

won't have ___ to wait an - y long - er, I've got to ___ be

strong - er.

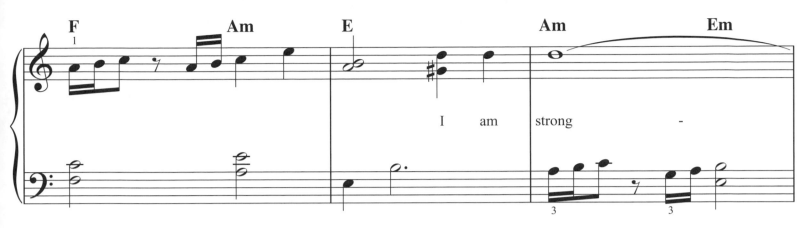

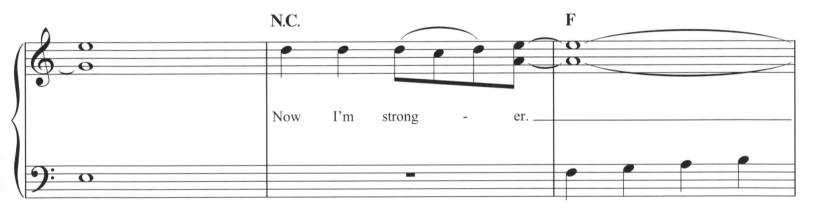

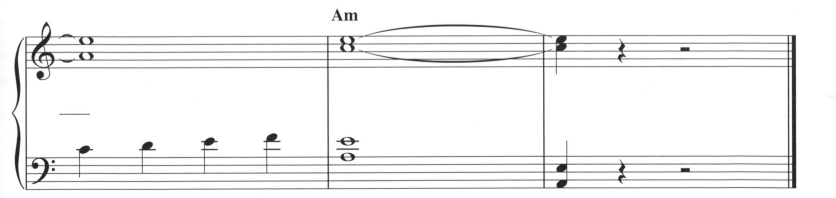

ALL THAT MATTERS

Words and Music by ELIOT KENNEDY
and GARY BARLOW

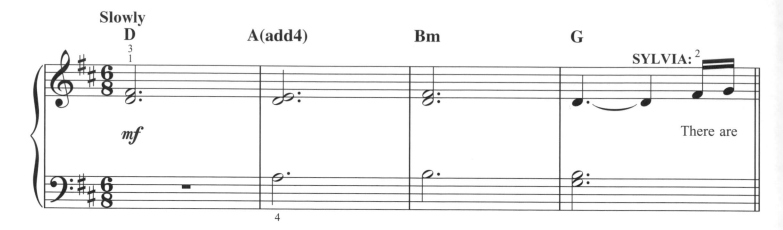

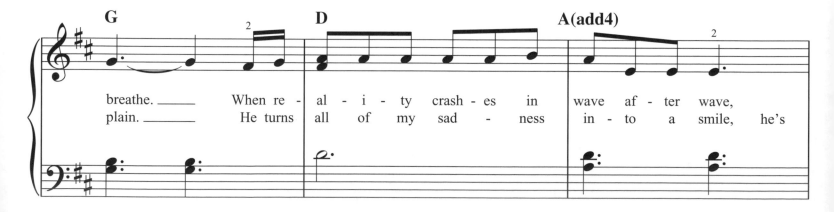

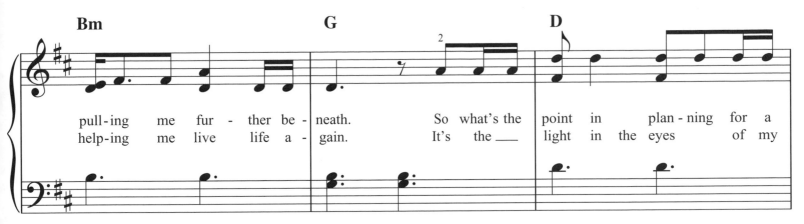

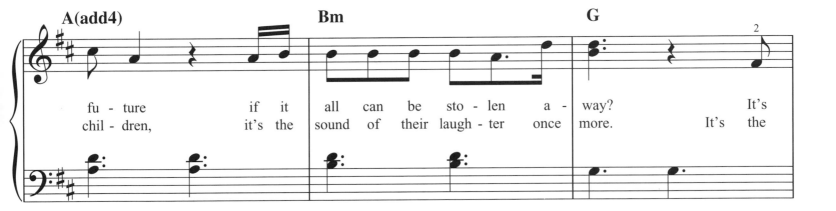

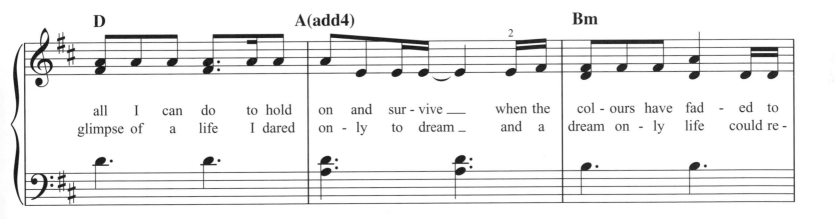

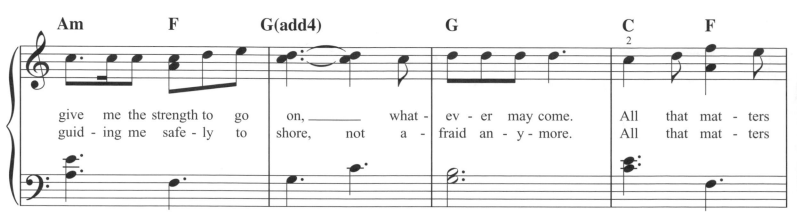

give me the strength to go on, _____ what - ev - er may come. All that mat - ters
guid - ing me safe - ly to shore, not a - fraid an - y - more. All that mat - ters

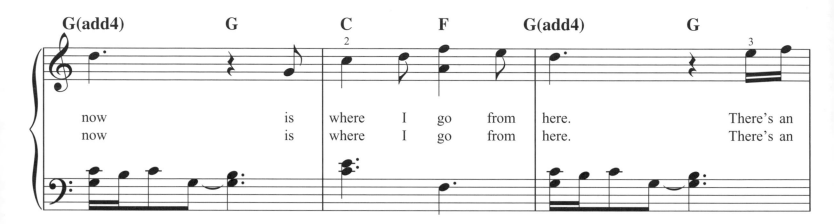

now   is   where   I   go   from   here.   There's an
now   is   where   I   go   from   here.   There's an

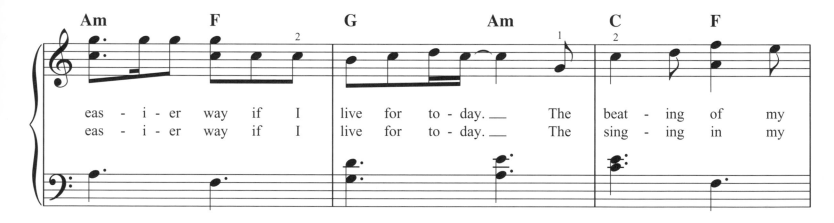

eas - i - er way if I live for to - day. __ The beat - ing of my
eas - i - er way if I live for to - day. __ The sing - ing in my

heart   is   all   that   mat - ters. __
heart   is   all   that   He makes

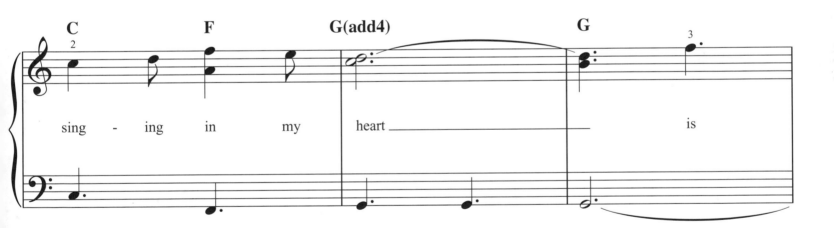

NEVERLAND

Words and Music by ELIOT KENNEDY
and GARY BARLOW

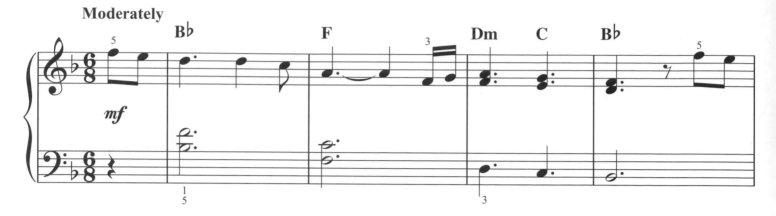

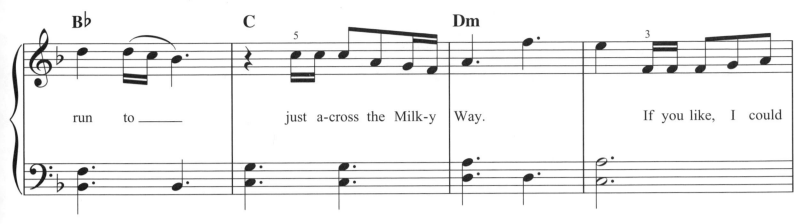

run to _____   just a-cross the Milk-y Way.   If you like, I could

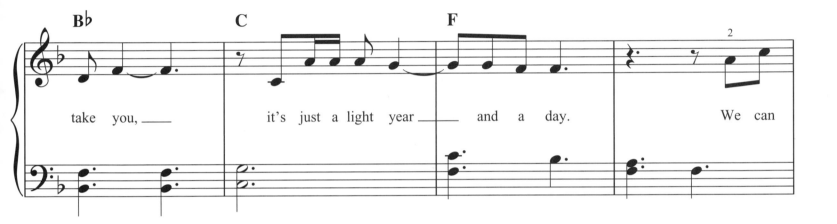

take you, _____   it's just a light year _____ and a day.   We can

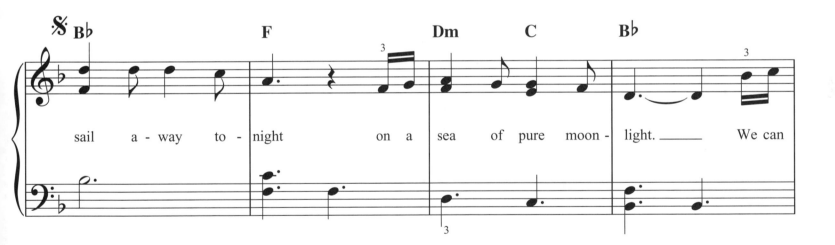

sail a - way to - night   on a sea of pure moon - light. _____ We can

nav - i - gate the   stars to bring us back   home. _____   In a

place so far a - way we'll be young, that's how we'll stay. _____ Ev -'ry

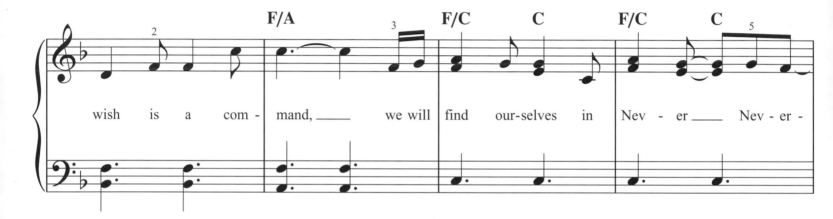

wish is a com - mand, _____ we will find our-selves in Nev - er _____ Nev-er-

To Coda ⊕

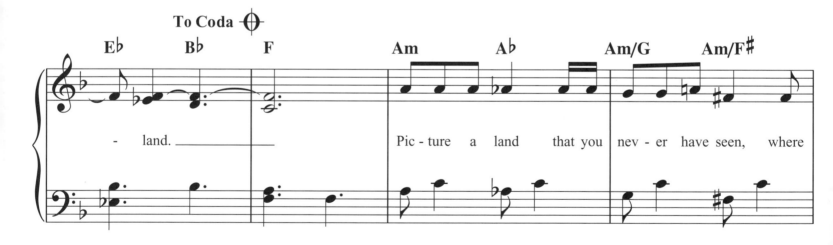

- land. _____ Pic - ture a land that you nev - er have seen, where

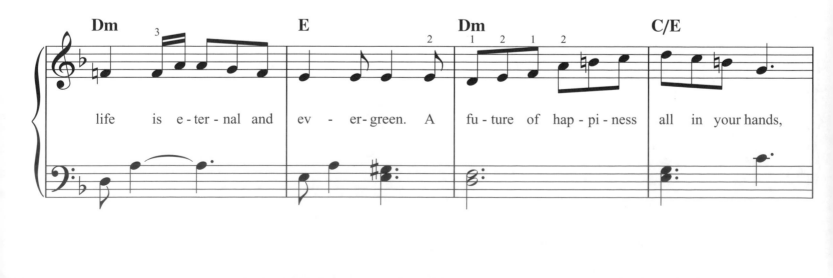

life is e - ter - nal and ev - er-green. A fu - ture of hap - pi - ness all in your hands,

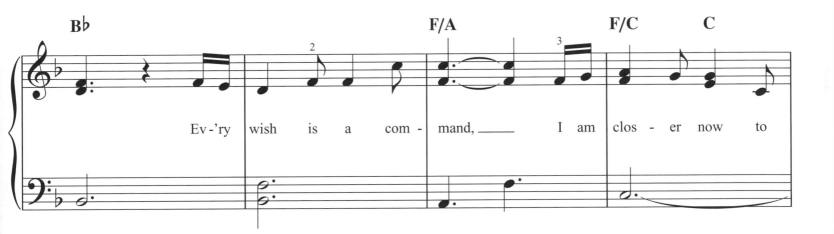

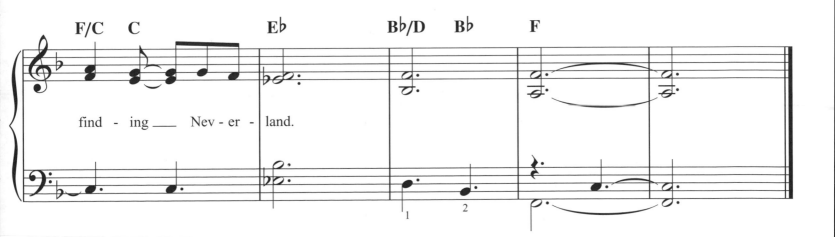

CIRCUS OF YOUR MIND

Words and Music by ELIOT KENNEDY
and GARY BARLOW

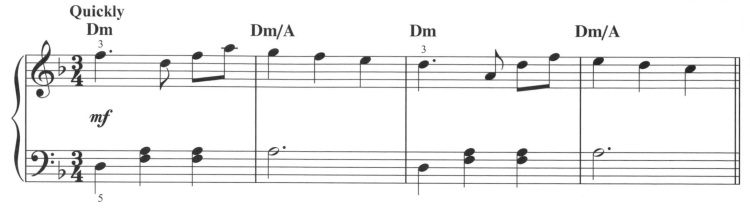

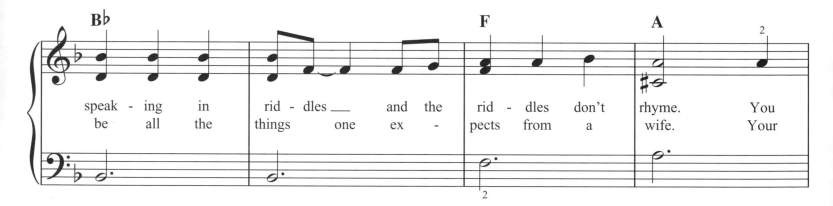

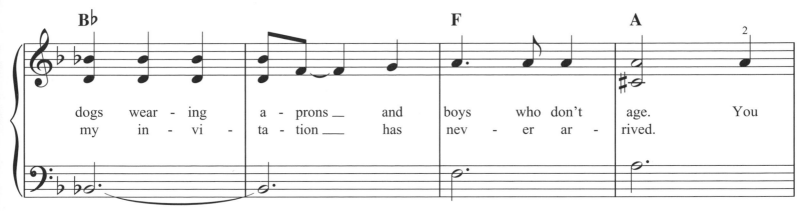

dogs wear - ing   a - prons __ and   boys who don't   age.   You
my in - vi - ta - tion __ has   nev - er ar - rived.

say I will a - dore   it   but I'm pay - ing __ for it.   A
Dar - ling, though you try __   you can - not de - ny   she's

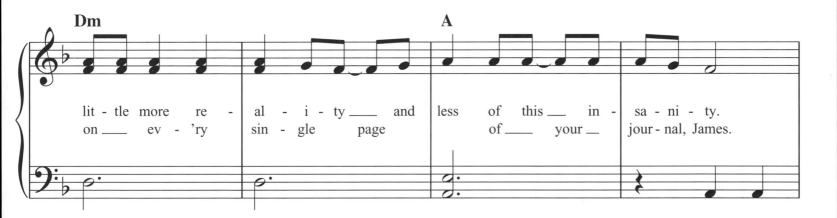

lit - tle more re - al - i - ty __ and less   of this __ in - sa - ni - ty.
on __ ev - 'ry   sin - gle page   of __ your __ jour - nal, James.

How'm I gon - na face   it?   Such   a   dis - grace,   yet
Now we have to face   it,   such   a   dis - grace,   yet

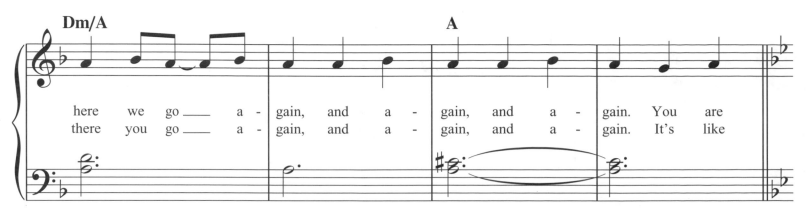

here we go ____ a - gain, and a - gain, and a - gain. You are
there you go ____ a - gain, and a - gain, and a - gain. It's like

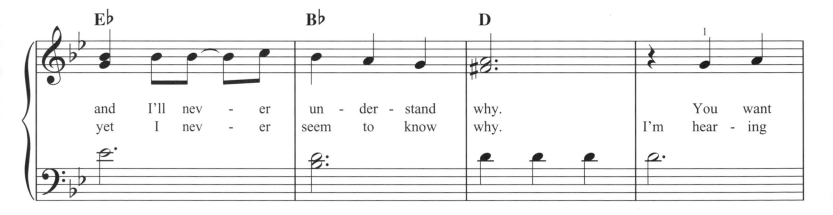

liv - ing on ____ a mer - ry - go - round, and 'round ____ you seem to go
liv - ing on ____ a mer - ry - go - round, and 'round ____ we seem to go

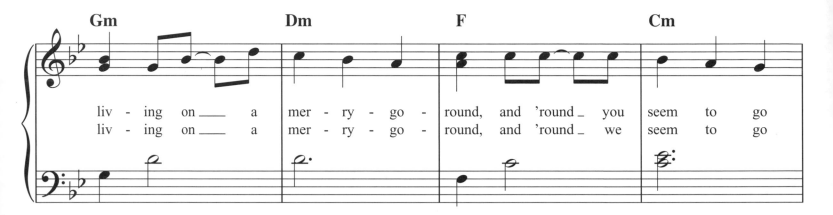

and I'll nev - er un - der - stand why. You want
yet I nev - er seem to know why. I'm hear - ing

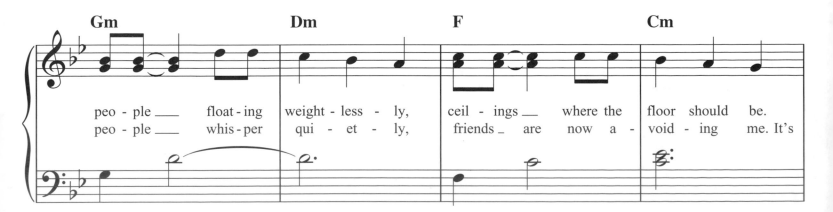

peo - ple ____ float - ing weight - less - ly, ceil - ings ____ where the floor should be.
peo - ple ____ whis - per qui - et - ly, friends ____ are now a - void - ing me. It's

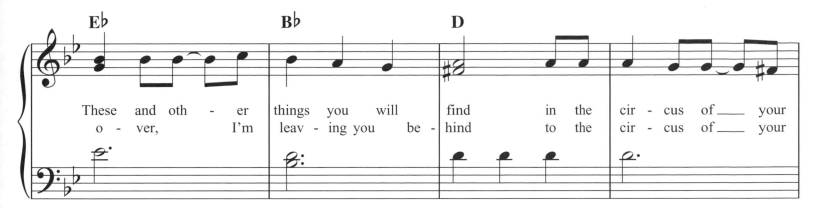

These and oth - er things you will find in the cir - cus of ___ your
o - ver, I'm leav - ing you be - hind to the cir - cus of ___ your

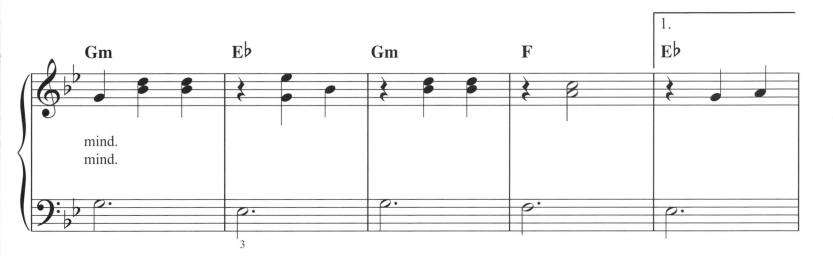

mind.
mind.

1.

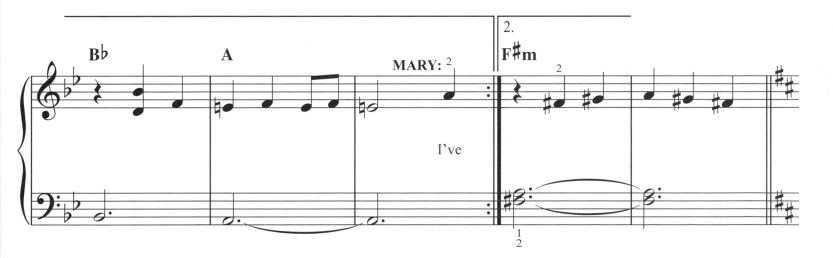

MARY:
I've

2.

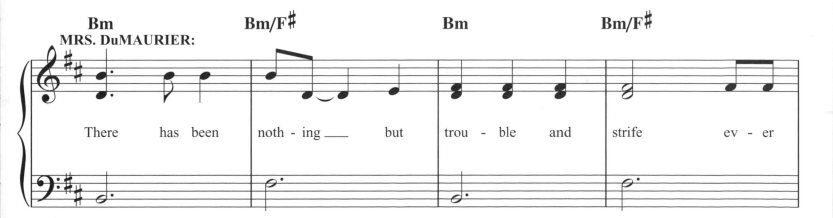

MRS. DuMAURIER:
There has been noth - ing ___ but trou - ble and strife ev - er

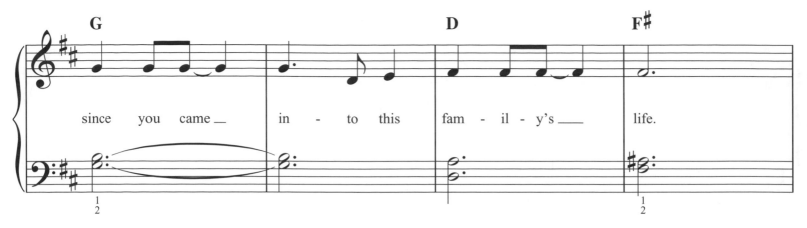

since you came ___ in - to this fam - il - y's ___ life.

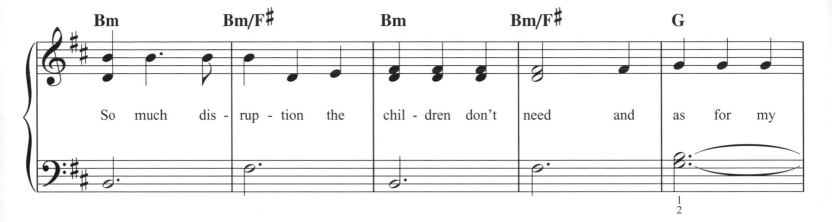

So much dis - rup - tion the chil - dren don't need and as for my

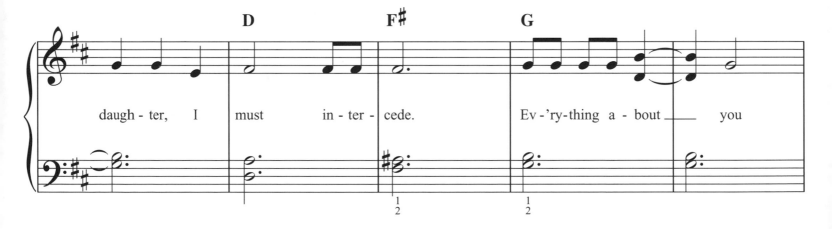

daugh - ter, I must in - ter - cede. Ev -'ry-thing a - bout ___ you

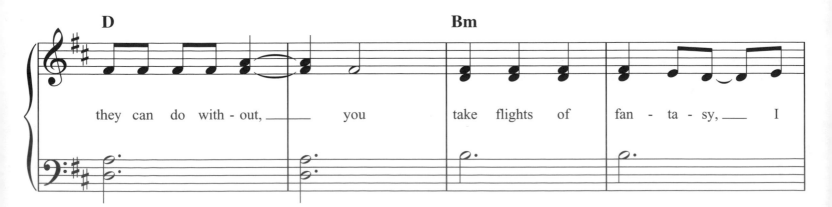

they can do with - out, ___ you take flights of fan - ta - sy, ___ I

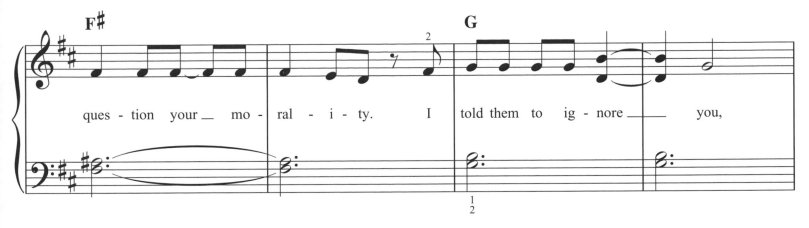

ques - tion your _ mo - ral - i - ty. I told them to ig - nore _____ you,

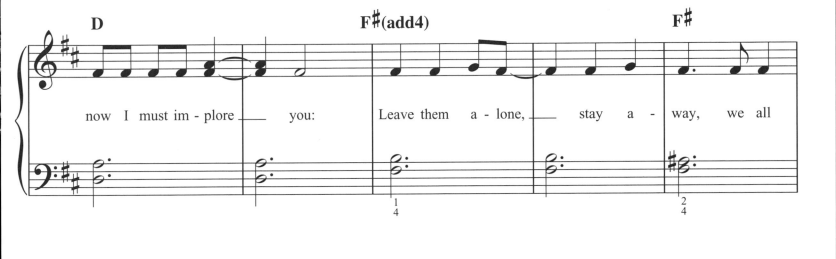

now I must im - plore _____ you: Leave them a - lone, ___ stay a - way, we all

know you are liv - ing on ___ a mer - ry - go - round, and 'round _ you

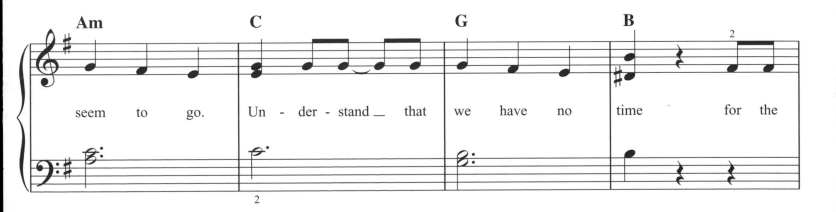

seem to go. Un - der - stand _ that we have no time for the

42

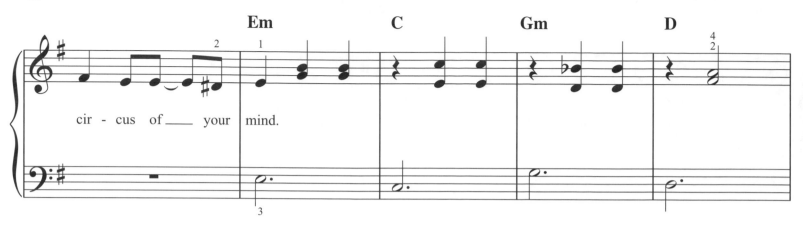

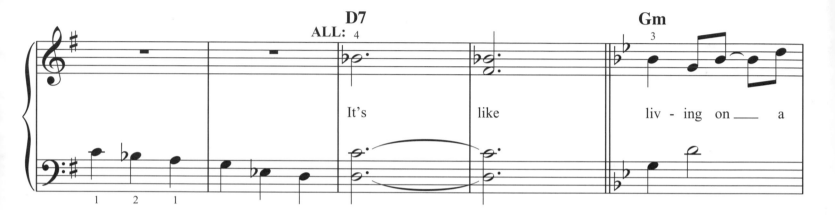

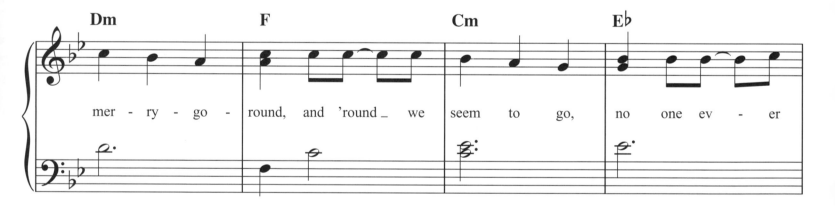

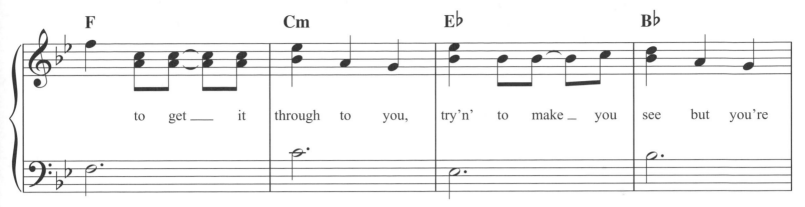

to get ___ it through to you, try'n' to make ___ you see but you're

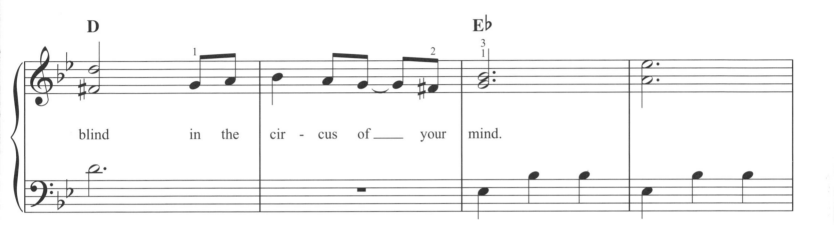

blind in the cir - cus of ___ your mind.

In the

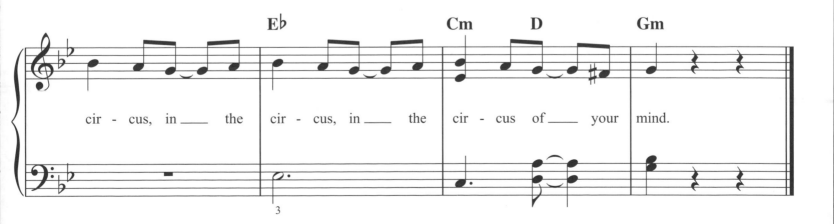

cir - cus, in ___ the cir - cus, in ___ the cir - cus of ___ your mind.

WHAT YOU MEAN TO ME

Words and Music by ELIOT KENNEDY
and GARY BARLOW

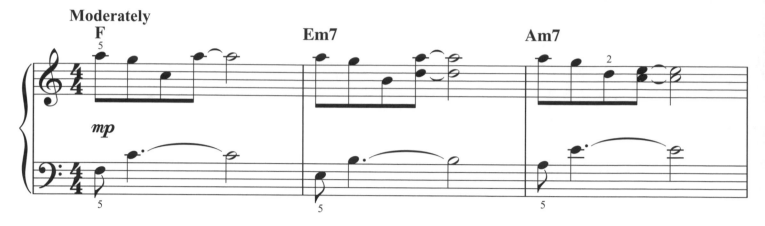

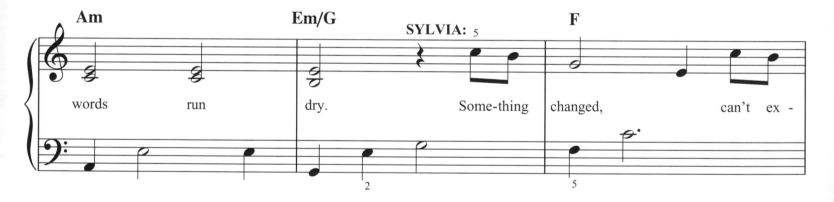

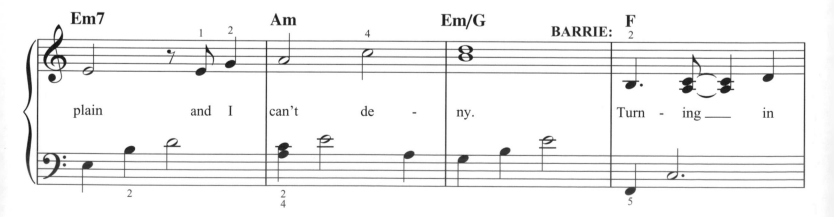

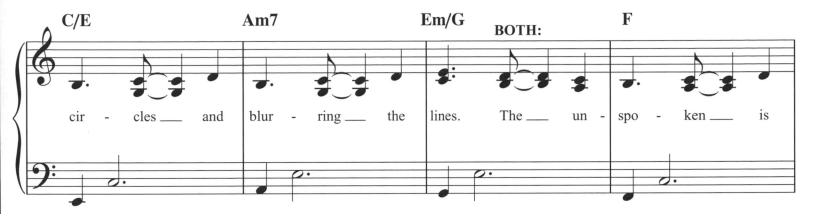

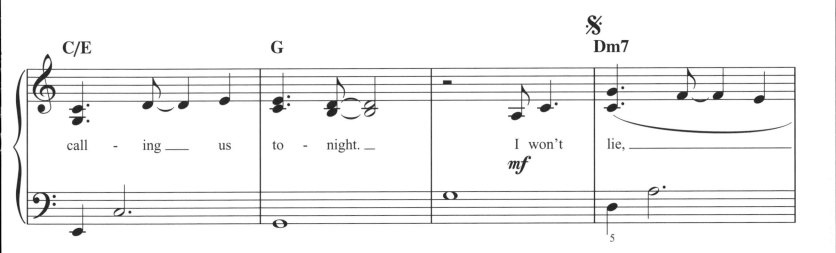

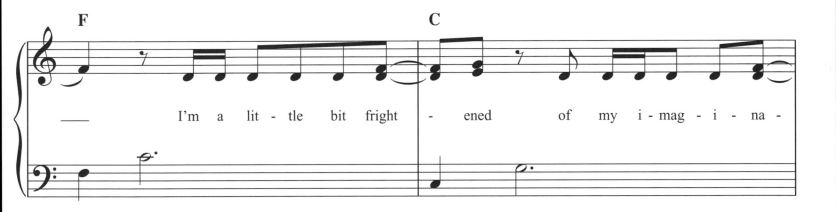

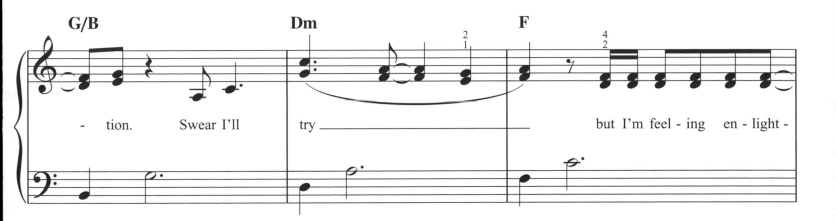

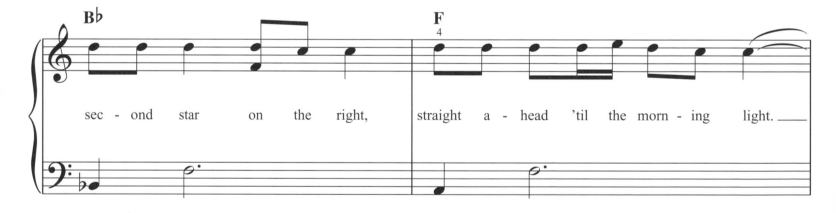

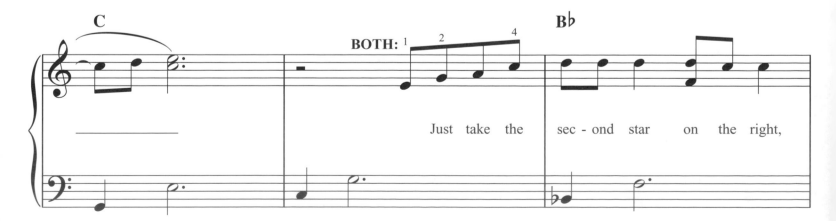

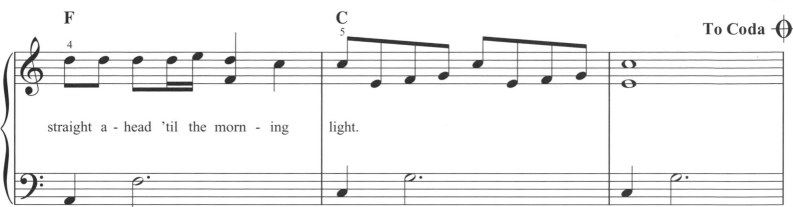

To Coda

straight a - head 'til the morn - ing | light.

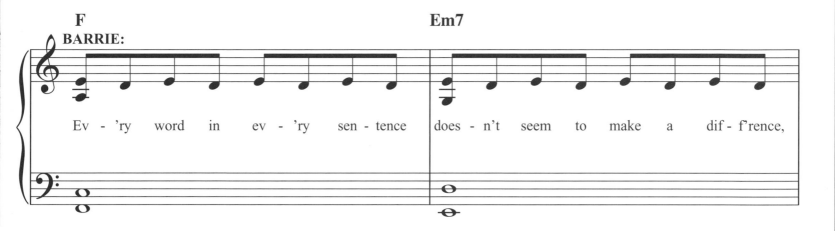

BARRIE:

Ev - 'ry word in ev - 'ry sen - tence | does - n't seem to make a dif - f'rence,

SYLVIA:

noth - ing can ex - plain just what you | mean to me. | Ev - 'ry shape and all the col - ours,

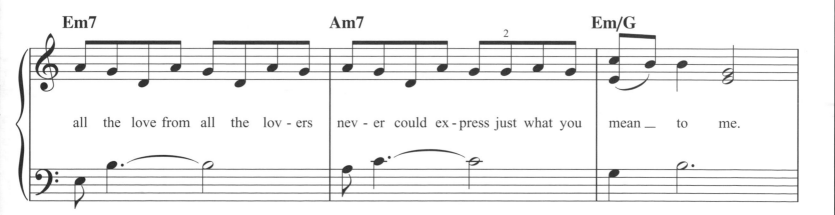

all the love from all the lov - ers | nev - er could ex - press just what you | mean __ to me.

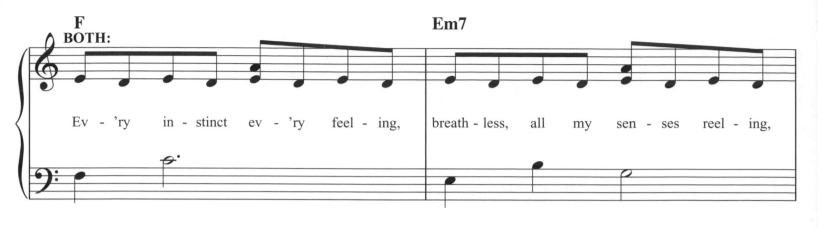

Ev - 'ry in - stinct ev - 'ry feel - ing, breath - less, all my sen - ses reel - ing,

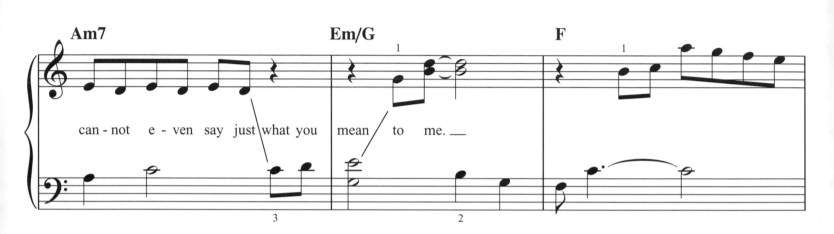

can - not e - ven say just what you mean to me. __

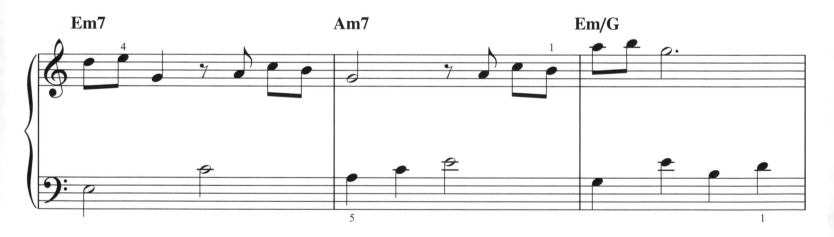

Em/G

F

C/E

Turn - ing ___ in cir - cles ___ and

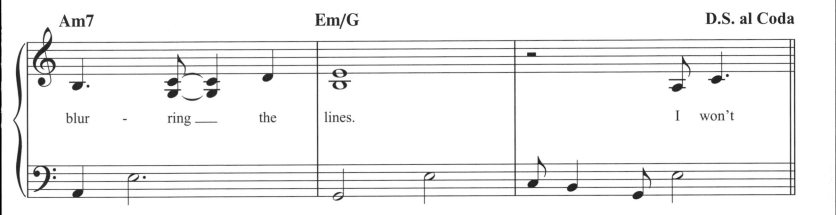

Am7

Em/G

D.S. al Coda

blur - ring ___ the lines.

I won't

CODA Slower
Fmaj7

C/E

Ev - 'ry star that's ev - er fall - en knows the way to where we're go - ing,

Am

Fsus2

C(add9)

now I real - ly know just what you mean to me.

PLAY

Words and Music by ELIOT KENNEDY
and GARY BARLOW

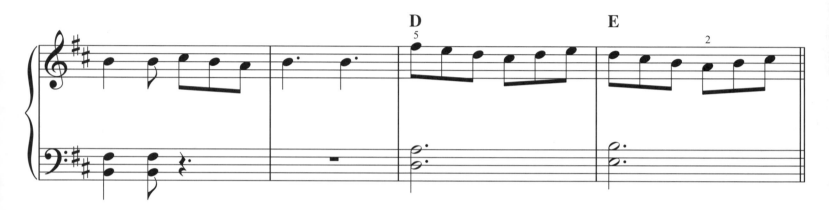

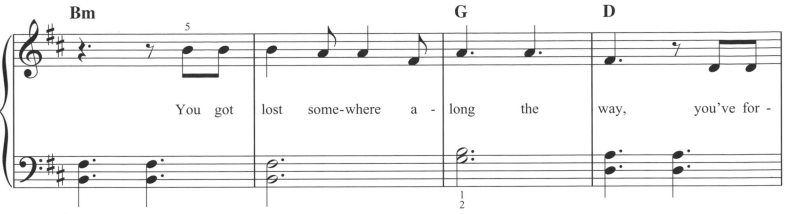

You got lost some-where a - long the way, you've for -

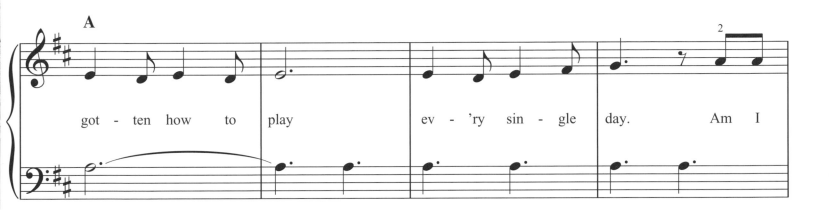

got - ten how to play ev - 'ry sin - gle day. Am I

right?

I re - mem - ber back when I was just a boy, I

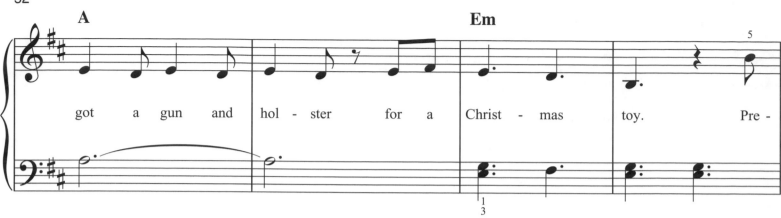

got a gun and hol - ster for a Christ - mas toy. Pre -

tend - ing to be a cow - boy _____ was the ver - y best, 'cause

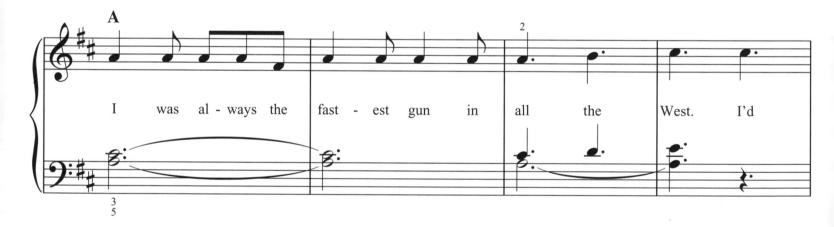

I was al - ways the fast - est gun in all the West. I'd

play, play, re - mem - ber like it was yes - ter - day.

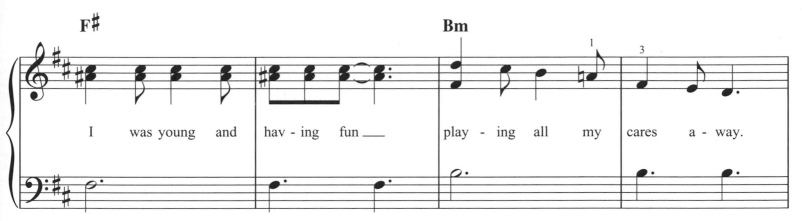

F#   Bm

I was young and hav - ing fun ___ play - ing all my cares a - way.

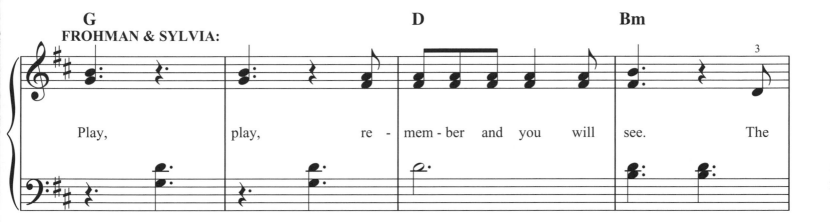

G   D   Bm

FROHMAN & SYLVIA:

Play, play, re - mem - ber and you will see. The

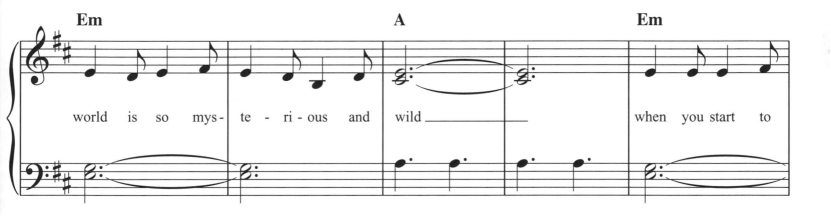

Em   A   Em

world is so mys - te - ri - ous and wild ___ when you start to

A   F#   Bm

see it through the eyes of a child. ___

54

Mr. Cromer. Surely you must have a childhood memory?

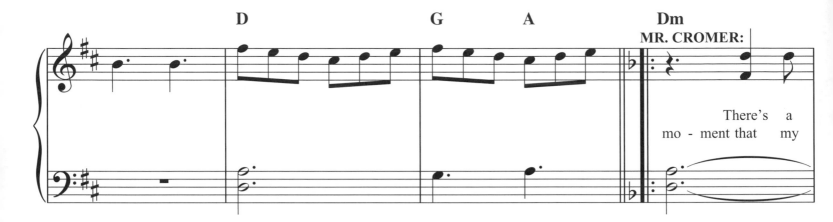

MR. CROMER:

There's a mo - ment that my

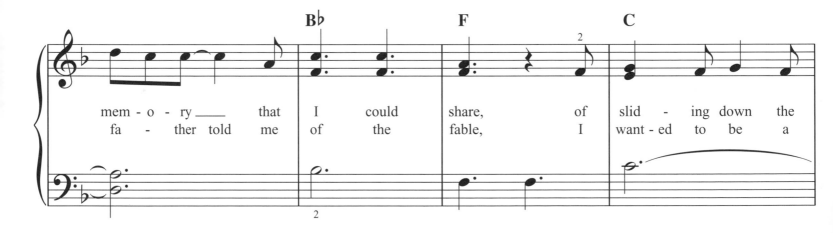

mem - o - ry _____ that I could share, of slid - ing down the
fa - ther told me of the fable, I want - ed to be a

ba - nis - ter of our old stairs. On - ly for a
knight of the King's Round Table. A sauce - pan on my

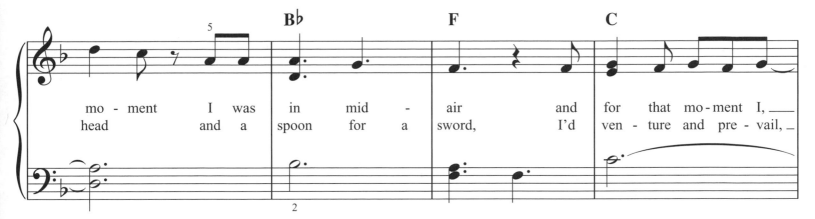

moment I was in mid - air and for that mo-ment I, ___
head and a spoon for a sword, I'd ven - ture and pre - vail, ___

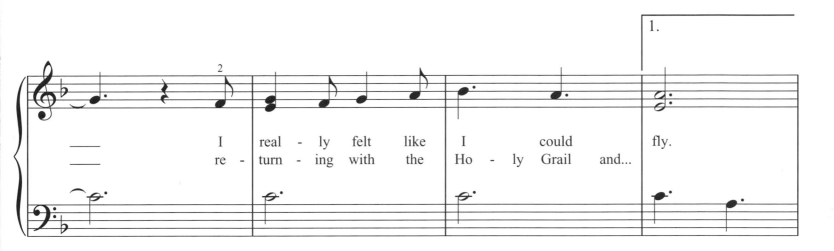

___ I real - ly felt like I could fly.
___ re - turn - ing with the Ho - ly Grail and...

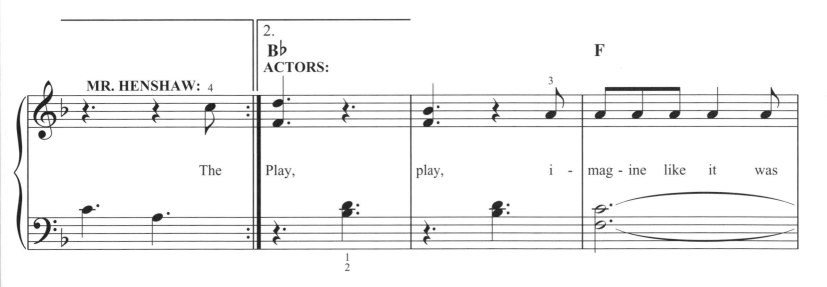

MR. HENSHAW:
The Play,

2.
B♭
ACTORS:
play, i - mag-ine like it was

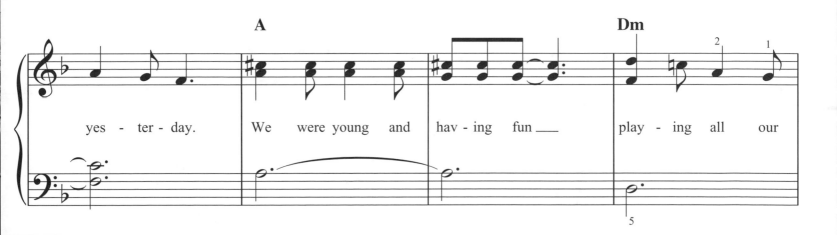

yes - ter - day. We were young and hav - ing fun ___ play - ing all our

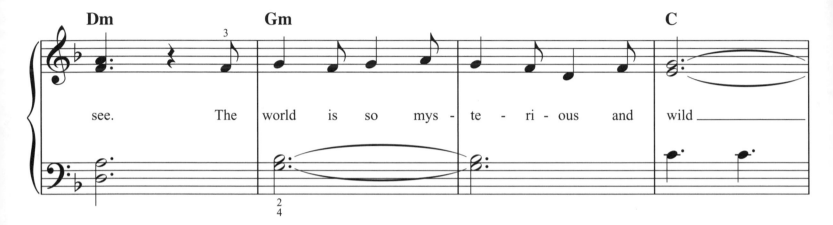

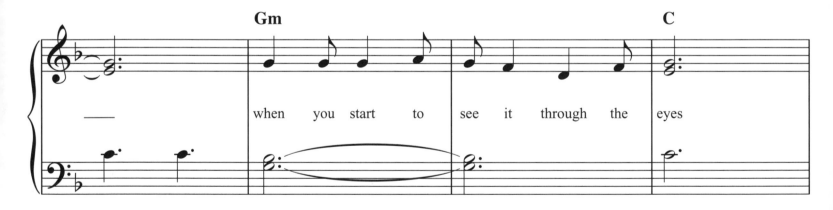

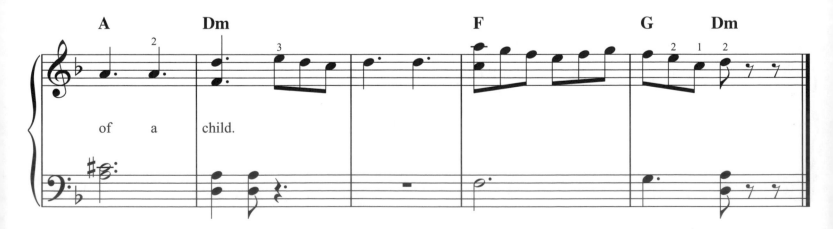

WE'RE ALL MADE OF STARS

Words and Music by ELIOT KENNEDY
and GARY BARLOW

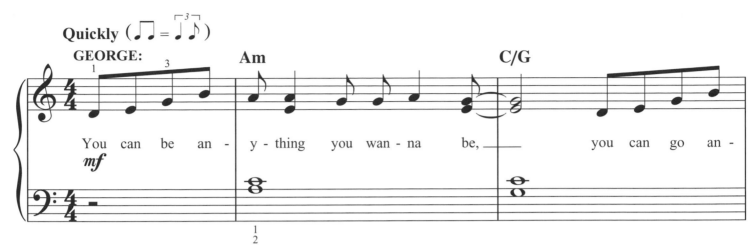

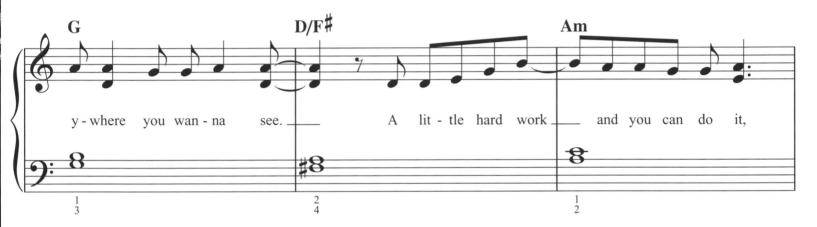

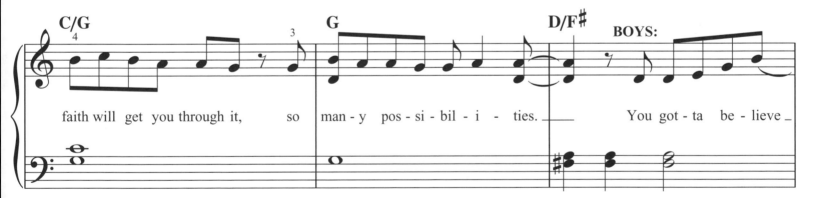

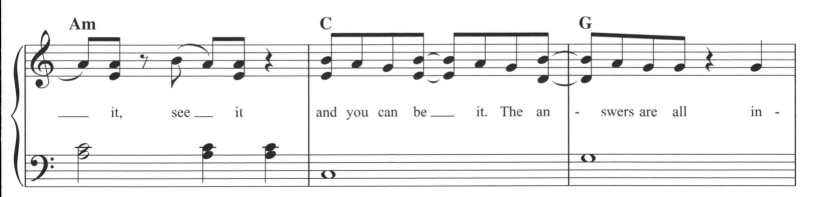

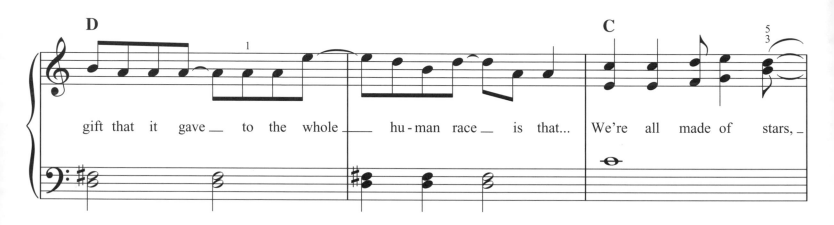

go where you like, be who you wan - na be. _

GEORGE: If a doc - tor could save _ on - ly just _ one life _ from pain _

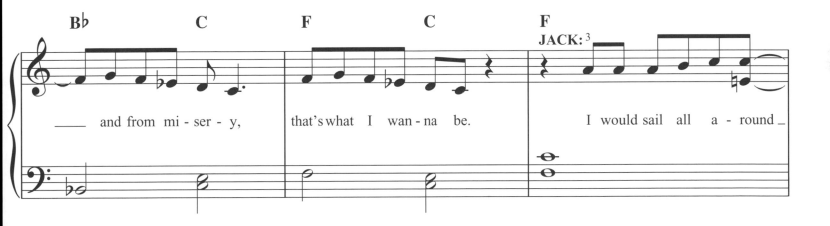

_ and from mi - ser - y, that's what I wan - na be. JACK: I would sail all a - round _

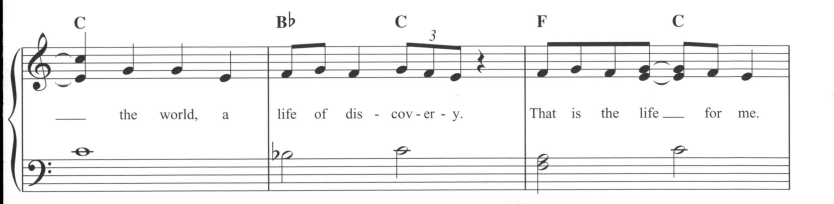

_ the world, a life of dis - cov - er - y. That is the life _ for me.

Am **D** **G**

PETER: If I could write ev-'ry sin - gle day I _____ would write all my cares ____

C **F** **C** **C/D** **D**

____ a - way. ___ I'd be lead-ing a dif - f'rent life. A MICHAEL: won-der-ful life! __

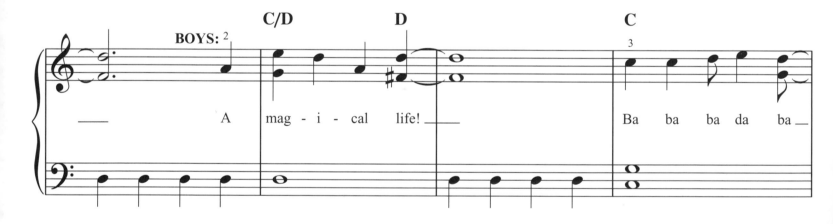

C/D **D** **C**

BOYS: ____ A mag - i - cal life! ____ Ba ba ba da ba __

G **B♭** **F** **C**

__ ba ba __ da. Ba ba ba da ba __ ba ba __ da. Ba ba ba da ba __

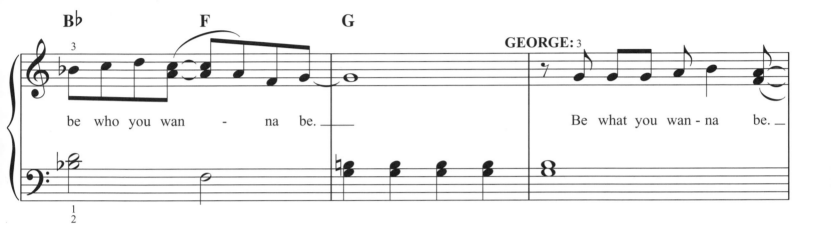

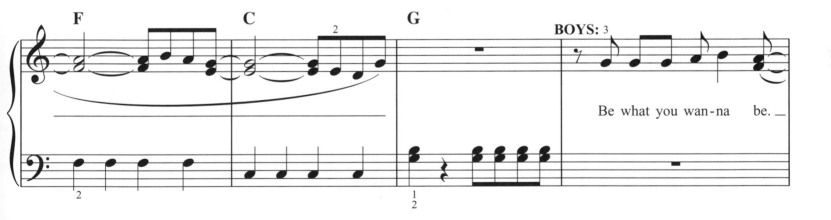

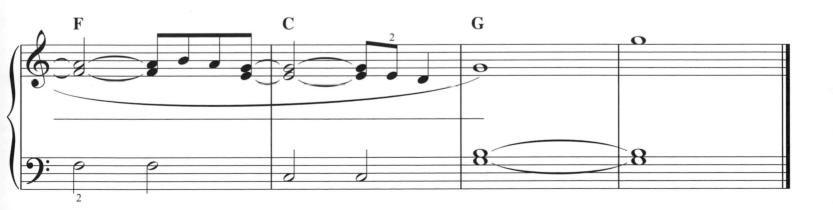

WHEN YOUR FEET DON'T TOUCH THE GROUND

Words and Music by ELIOT KENNEDY
and GARY BARLOW

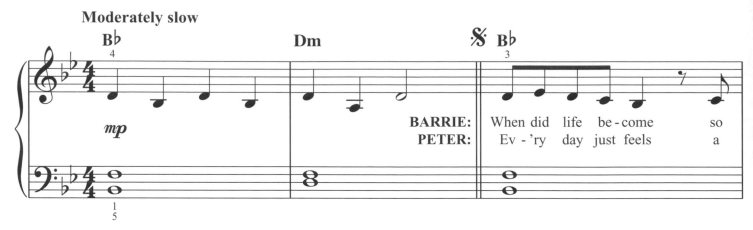

BARRIE: When did life be-come so
PETER: Ev-'ry day just feels a

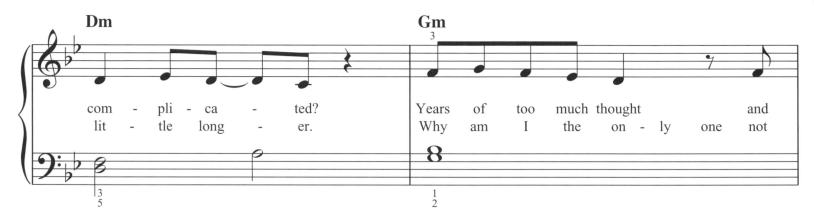

com - pli - ca - ted?
lit - tle long - er.

Years of too much thought and
Why am I the on - ly one not

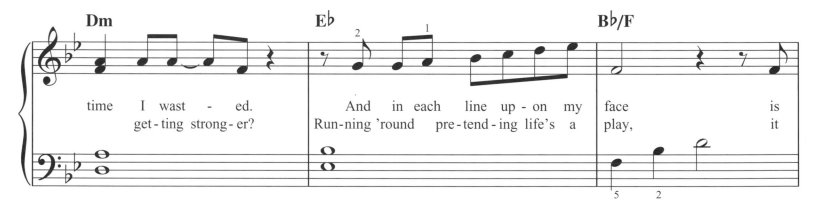

time I wast - ed.
get - ting strong - er?

And in each line up - on my
Run - ning 'round pre - tend - ing life's a

face is
play, it

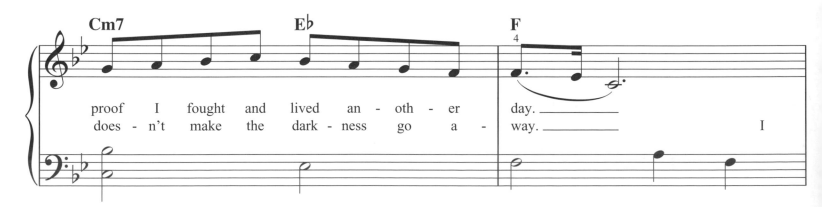

proof I fought and lived an - oth - er
does - n't make the dark - ness go a -

day. _____
way. _____ I

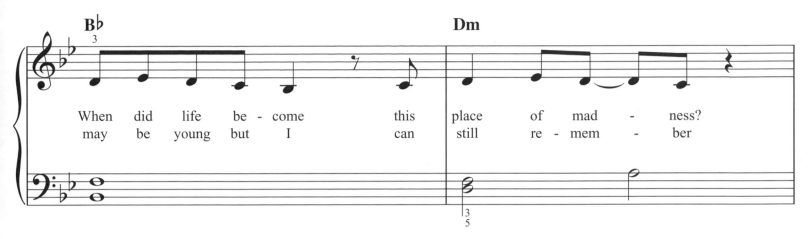

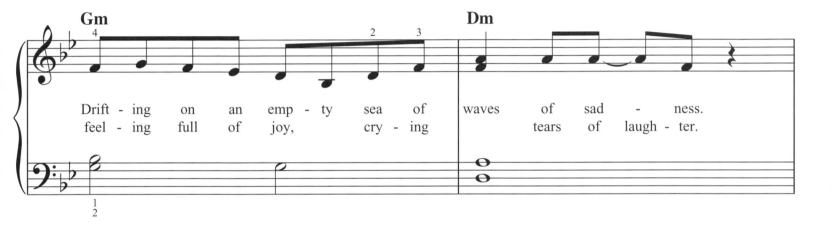

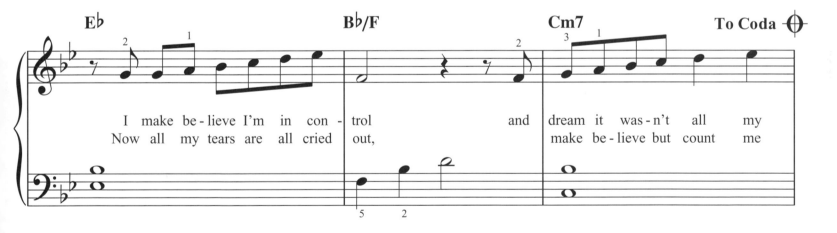

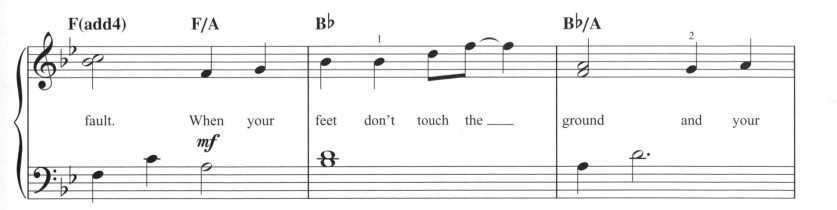

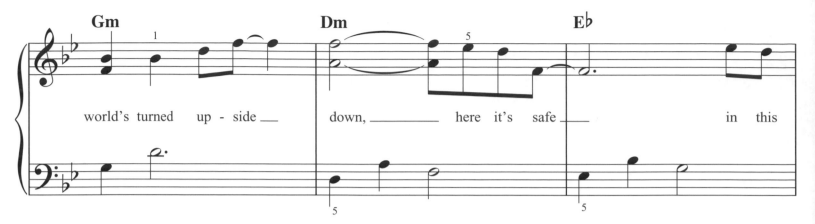

world's turned up - side __ down, _____ here it's safe __ in this

place a - bove the clouds. _____ When your feet don't touch the

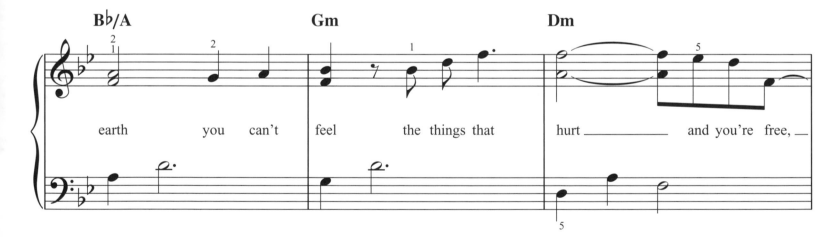

earth you can't feel the things that hurt _____ and you're free, __

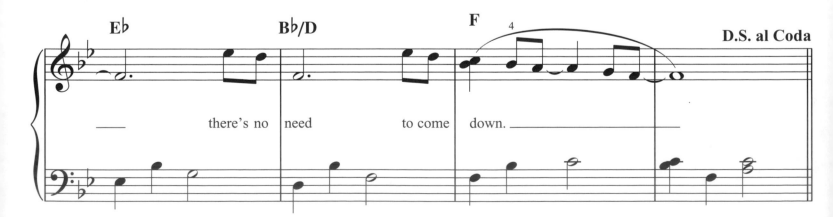

__ there's no need to come down. _____

D.S. al Coda

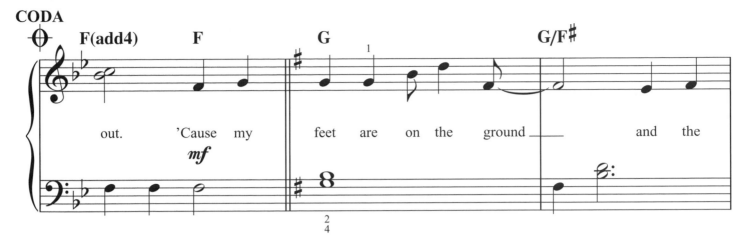

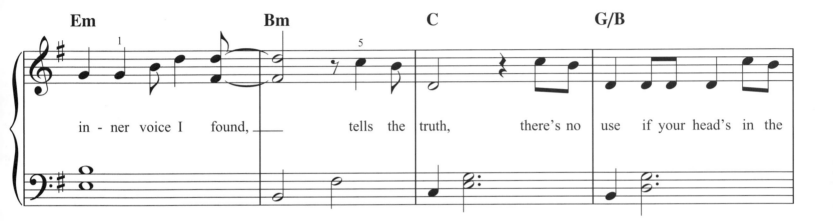

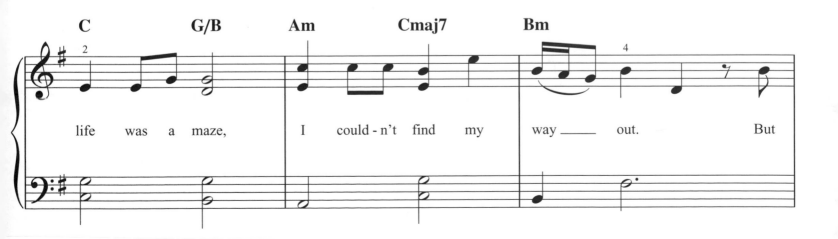

what I say is true,   you'll be a-mazed,   make be-lieve and you   will

find out that it's true. ___
PETER: I know what is   true.   When your   feet don't touch the
mf

ground   and your   world's turned up-side   down, _____ here it's safe ___

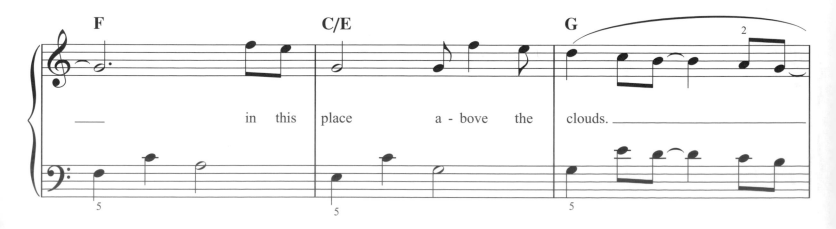

___   in this place   a-bove the   clouds. ___

67

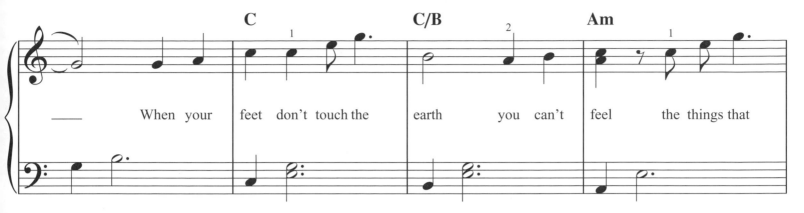

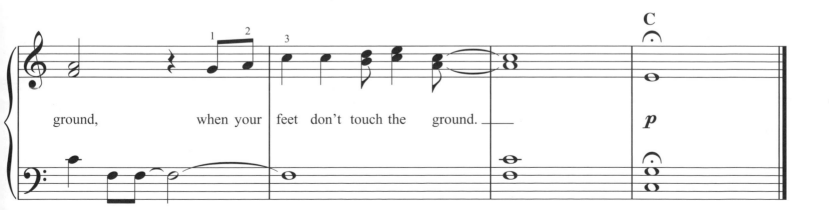

FINALE

Words and Music by ELIOT KENNEDY
and GARY BARLOW

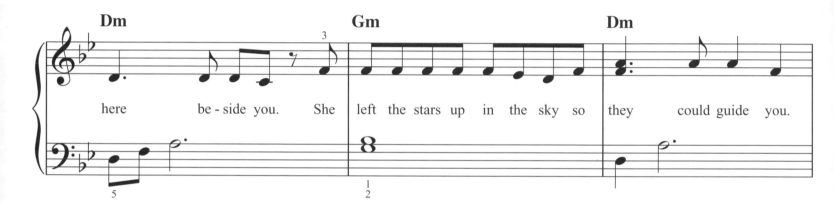

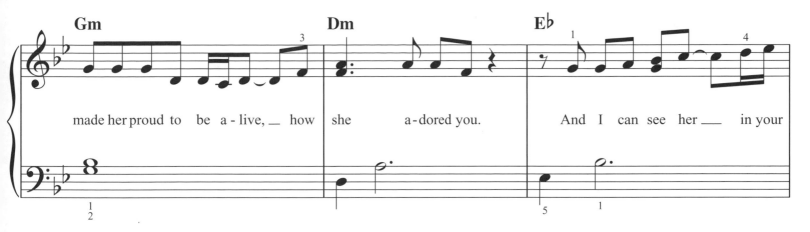

made her proud to be a-live, __ how she a-dored you. And I can see her __ in your

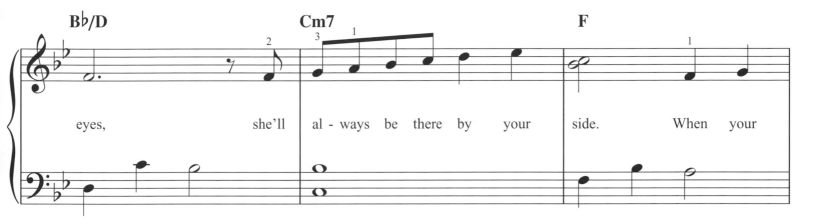

eyes, she'll al-ways be there by your side. When your

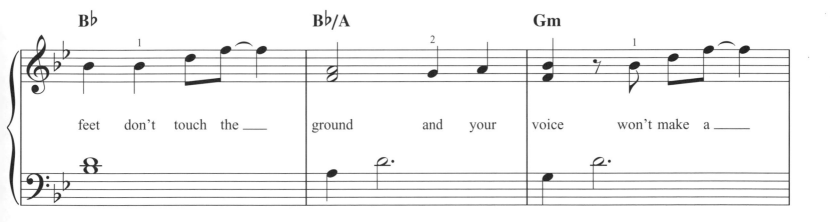

feet don't touch the __ ground and your voice won't make a __

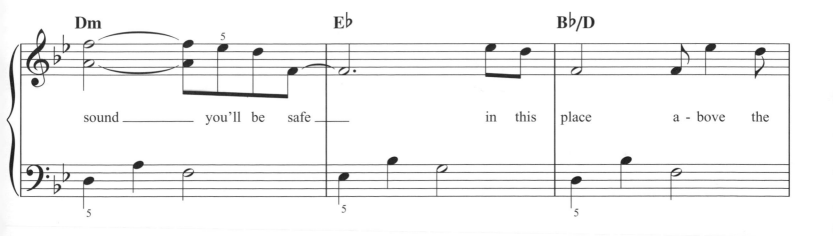

sound __ you'll be safe __ in this place a-bove the

70

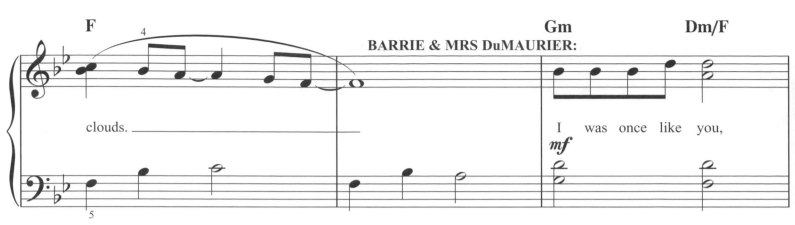

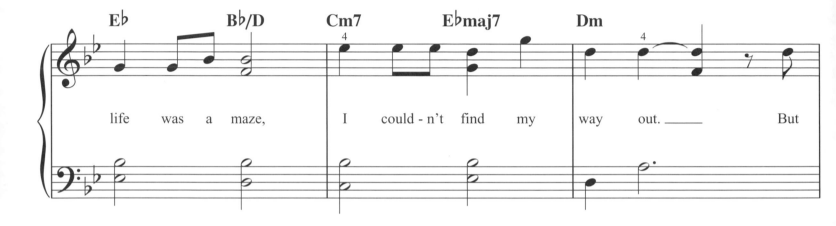

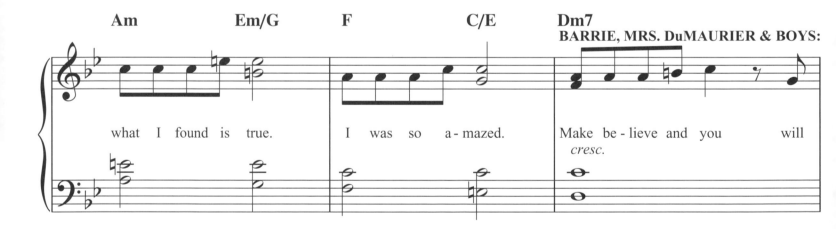

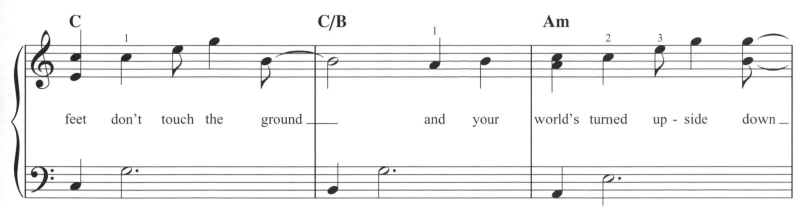

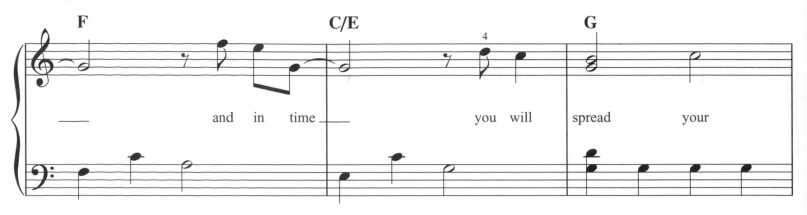

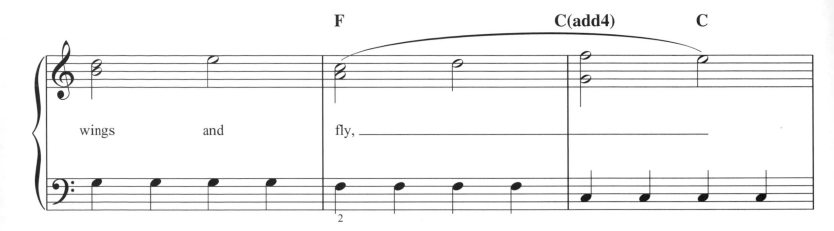

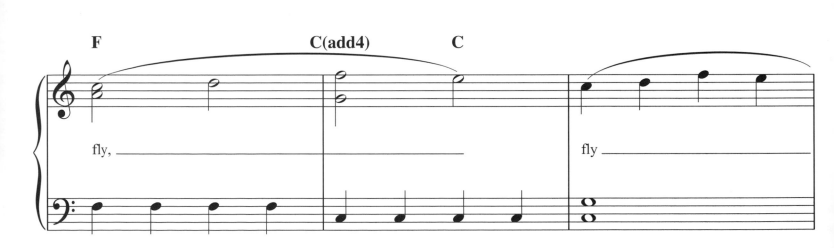

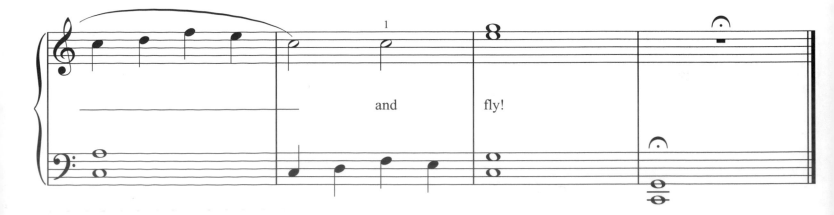